BOOK 2

Another Page

An instructional program for adults who want to improve reading comprehension skills.

The Kentucky Network

Pages 26-27—Passage 9 is an excerpt from a copyrighted booklet, "Dollars and Sense," prepared by the Advertising Council for its anti-inflation campaign.
Page 66—Dictionary entry is reprinted by permission from Webster's New Collegiate Dictionary @1981 by G. & C. Merriam Company, Publishers of the Merriam-Webster Dictionaries.
Pages 65, 85—Excerpts are from *Reader's Guide to Periodical Literature*, vol. 80, no. 15 (Nov. 10, 1980), @ 1980 by the H.W. Wilson Company. Material reproduced by permission of the publisher.
Pages 67-68, 74-75—Encyclopedia entries are reprinted courtesy of Columbia University Press from *The New Columbia Encyclopedia*, @ 1975 by Columbia University Press.
Pages 69-70, 70-71, 71-72—Excerpts are reprinted from *The Medicine Show*, by Consumers Union, @ 1977 by Consumers Union of the United States.
Page 73—Excerpts are reprinted courtesy of McGraw-Hill Book Company from a bibliography in *The Consumer in American Society*, by Jack Taylor and Arch Troelstrup, @ 1974 by McGraw-Hill Book Company.
Pages 75-76, 78-81, 86-88, 88-89—Excerpts are reprinted courtesy of Consumer News, Inc., from *Help: The Indispensable Almanac of Consumer Information*, edited by Arthur E. Rowse, @ 1980 by Consumer News, Inc.
Page 76—Excerpt is reprinted by permission of Macmillan Publishing Co., Inc., from a bibliography in *Fundamentals of Normal Nutrition*, 2nd edition, by C.H. Robinson, @ 1973 by Macmillan Publishing Co., Inc.
Page 78—Excerpt is reprinted from the table of contents in *The Great American Auto Repair Robbery*, by Donald A. Randall and Arthur Glickman, @ 1972 by Donald A. Randall and Arthur Glickman. By permission of Brandt & Brandt, Co.

Another Page Book 2
This book accompanies programs 4-6 of the *Another Page* television series, produced by KET, The Kentucky Network.

WRITER: Guy Mendes
EDITORS/CONSULTANTS: Brian Schenk, Peter Fondulas, Dennis Mendyk, Ann Davidson-Serrão, Jack Ericson, Helen Giuliano-Solana, Elliott Lethbridge, and Kayreitha Smalls, Cambridge Book Company.

ISBN 0-910475-47-4 1 2 3 4 5

Much of the material in this book originally appeared in *Another Page Practical Reading*, © 1981, Kentucky Authority for Educational Television.

How To Use the *Another Page* Videotapes and Student Workbooks

Another Page is a series of 15 half-hour video lessons and five student workbooks. It is designed for new adult readers who have mastered the basic reading skills and are ready to begin work on developing comprehension and vocabulary.

Each ***Another Page*** video lesson covers a particular reading comprehension skill and introduces new vocabulary words. Reading motivation is also provided within each program. The ***Another Page*** workbook chapters complement the video lessons with additional explanatory material and practice exercises to reinforce the reading skills and vocabulary introduced in the video lessons.

Another Page may be used by students working independently or in groups. Because the series design is based on progressive skill development and uses two continuing dramatic plot lines, students should begin with Program/Workbook Chapter 1 and move through the series in numerical sequence.

Students and instructors may use the ***Another Page*** video lessons in a variety of settings: from open broadcast into the student's home or into the learning center, or on a videocassette recorder (VCR) in the student's home or in the learning center. Most instructors prefer working with ***Another Page*** using a VCR, since that method offers both instructor and student a more interactive approach.

In general, television learning is most effective when the following stages are observed by students and tutors:

1. **Preparation**—Students complete a simple goal-setting activity to help them know what to look for in the video lesson.
2. **Participation**—After the students view the video lesson, the instructor helps them do workbook exercises, writing assignments, or other activities to reinforce the skills presented in the program.
3. **Practice**—Instructors identify the specific learning needs of the students and provide materials for practicing the necessary skills.

The ***Another Page*** workbooks are especially helpful in providing practice activities that will help students master the skills presented in the video lessons. Each workbook chapter is divided into five parts:

1. Preview of the video lesson and new vocabulary
2. First Intermission—reading passages and questions
3. Second Intermission—reading passages and questions
4. After the Show—vocabulary and reading skills review
5. More Pages—supplemental reading passages in TV script format

Both the ***Another Page*** video lessons and the workbooks that accompany them can be used whole or in segments, depending on an individual student's needs and the instructional setting. Some instructors working with groups prefer to use the programs in class, watching and working with the video lesson as a group and assigning the workbook chapter afterward as homework. Other instructors use the ***Another Page*** materials to supplement work in the basal reader. ***Another Page*** also can be used by students who enjoy working on their own, either as enrichment or as an extension of classroom activities.

In addition to reading comprehension skills, ***Another Page*** offers students and instructors a rich variety of writing assignment ideas, discussion topics, and library research project ideas.

Contents

4

Making Inferences

In this unit, you will practice making inferences. When you make an inference, you assume, or figure out, something that is not directly stated in the passage. You will see that in order to make an inference, you must combine the facts and details in the passage with your own common sense.

Videotape Preview

The videotape you are about to watch is divided into three parts. In the first part, Darrell warns Mr. John about burglaries in Mr. John's neighborhood. Also in the first part, Rhonda sees an ad in the newspaper for a used car.

"The Inside Story," the second part of the tape, will give you practice in drawing conclusions and making inferences. You will see that when you draw conclusions and make inferences, you figure out things about the passage that are not directly stated in the passage.

In the third part of the tape, Mr. John, after a close call with an intruder, uses his reading skill to learn about burglar-proofing his home. Also in the third part, Candy and Rhonda do a bit of reading about cars and realize that Rhonda's new car is a lemon.

As you watch the first part of the tape, try to answer the following questions:

- How do you think Darrell feels about hearing Mr. John's boxing stories?
- What does Mr. John infer about the picture in the newspaper?
- What details in the picture help Mr. John figure out what happened in the picture?
- How do you think Mr. John feels about what Darrell has to say?
- From what Candy and Rhonda say, what can you infer about the price of Cadillacs and Continentals?
- From the information in the ad, what kind of shape do you think the car's body is in?
- How do you think Candy feels about Rhonda's eagerness to buy the car mentioned in the ad?

Vocabulary

The following words are used on the tape. Before you watch the tape or do any work in this unit, study the meanings of these words.

additives: ingredients that are added to foods in order to improve the quality of the food
*Many companies use **additives** that make foods look more appetizing.*

artificial: not natural; manmade
*Does that food contain **artificial** ingredients, or is it all-natural?*

burglary: the act of breaking into a home or building for the purpose of stealing valuables
*The police arrested the man they found in the warehouse and charged him with **burglary**.*

defy: to refuse to cooperate with or obey
*If you **defy** the orders of a superior, you could get into serious trouble.*

guarantee: an assurance of the quality of a product
I know that I can get my money back if anything goes wrong with the "Wonder Slicer": It came with a written, money-back ***guarantee.***

humidifier: a machine that adds moisture to the air
If the air in your home is too dry in the winter, you might consider buying a ***humidifier.***

humidity: the amount of moisture in the air
In the summer, when the ***humidity*** *is high, the air is hot and sticky.*

illusion: something that fools someone into believing what is not true
That woman was not really sawed in half; it was just an ***illusion.***

infection: the condition that results when a disease-producing substance enters the body
If an open wound is invaded by germs, you may get an ***infection.***

infer: to come to a conclusion based on evidence
From the look on his face, we could ***infer*** *that he had been offered the job.*

neutralizing: taking away the effect of
After ***neutralizing*** *the dangerous chemical, he assured the townspeople that the water was safe to drink.*

obsolete: no longer being used
Electrical ignition systems in cars have made the crank starter ***obsolete.***

ransacked: removed the valuables from
The burglars ***ransacked*** *the house, leaving her with nothing of value.*

repel: to drive away
The loud noise made by a burglar alarm is meant to ***repel*** *intruders.*

stabilizers: additives used to improve and maintain the quality of foods

__Stabilizers__ are used to prevent ice crystals from forming on foods.

strike plate: a metal fastening on a door frame into which the bolt of a lock fits

__Strike plates__ that are not fastened securely make it easy for a burglar to kick in the door.

symbol: something that stands for or suggests something else

*To many people, the lion is a **symbol** of courage.*

Watch Part 1

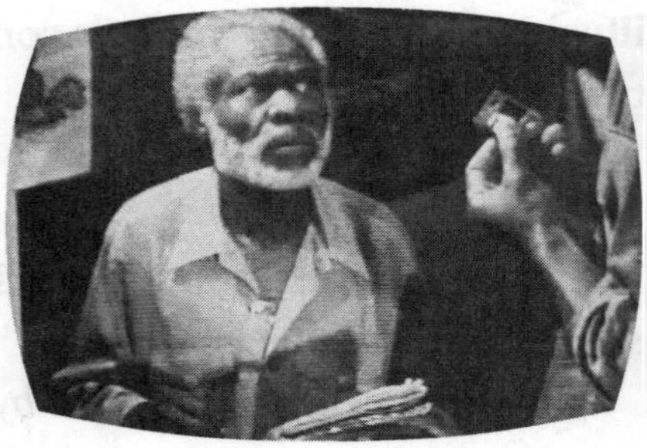

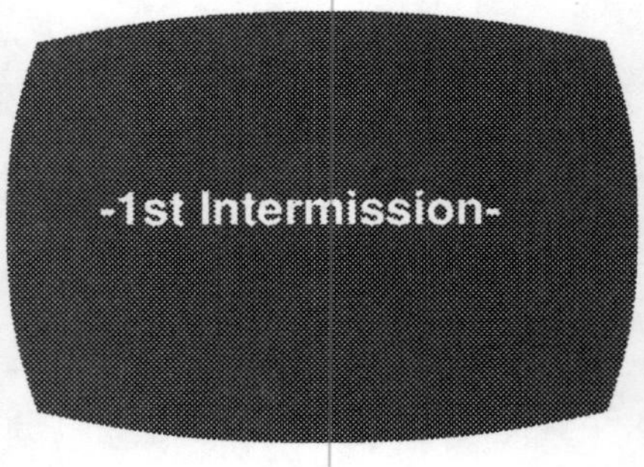

An inference is a guess that is based on evidence and your own common sense. When you make an inference, you assume something that is not directly stated.

Here's an example. It's a hot, humid summer evening. You're sitting in the living room, you have the window fan on full blast, and you're watching the baseball game on television. You have just put a load of dirty laundry in the washing machine, and you can hear the machine running.

Just as the pitcher gets into his windup, the television goes off. Not only that, but every light in the apartment goes off, the fan goes off, and you can hear the washing machine grind to a halt.

What happened? You guess, or infer, that either:

- you blew a fuse, or
- there has been a blackout

Which is correct? You look out the window. You notice that not a single light is on in any building outside. You also notice that all of the street lights are out. From this you can guess, or infer, that at least part of your neighborhood is experiencing a blackout.

In this example, you guessed, or inferred, what was going on from the evidence around you. No voice came from the sky and announced: "Attention—this is a blackout." Instead, you made an inference by:

- looking for evidence (all of the appliances go off at the same time, and no lights are on outside).
- using your common sense (you know that if all of the appliances go off at the same time, and if the lights go off in the buildings and streets around you, it means there has been a blackout).

Now that you know that an inference is a guess based on evidence and common sense, you probably have realized that you make inferences every day.

When you drive a car, you must make many inferences. Suppose you are driving to work on a two-lane road that is usually free of traffic. However, on this day the cars are backed up for what seems to be miles. You stretch your neck out the window and notice flashing red lights way up ahead. You guess, or infer, that there has been an accident on the road.

So, you're creeping along at a snail's pace when you notice a steady flow of steam coming from under the hood of a car up ahead. From this you infer that the car has overheated.

Next, you notice that the driver of the car directly behind the overheated car starts to change lanes without looking to see if there are any cars near him. And you notice that the man in the car alongside the car that is changing lanes also is not paying attention to the cars around him. You infer that unless one of the two drivers sees what is going on, there will be a slight collision. You honk your horn to try to warn them. But it is too late. Your inference was correct.

Now, aside from the accident up ahead and the overheated car, you are stuck behind the two cars that have collided. Based on the extent of the traffic jam and based on your past experience with situations like this, you infer that by the time this mess is cleaned up, you will be late for work.

In this example, you, the driver, were not directly told what was going on. There was no sign on the road saying, "This traffic jam is being caused by an accident on the road." The man in the car with the steam coming from under the hood did not jump out of his car and yell, "Look everyone, my car has overheated!" And no one yelled,"Look, those two cars are about to collide!"

Instead, you made inferences by:

(1) looking at the evidence

- flashing red lights and traffic on a usually traffic-free road
- steam coming from under the hood of a car
- two cars heading for each other with drivers who are not watching what they're doing

(2) using your common sense

- You know that when there is traffic on a usually traffic-free road, it means that something is wrong. Also, you know that flashing red lights usually belong to a police car or an ambulance and that these vehicles are often at the scene of an accident.
- You know that cars often overheat in heavy traffic and that steam coming from under the hood of a car is a sign that the car has overheated.
- You know that when two cars are headed for each other and the drivers are not paying attention, the two cars will collide.

The following questions are based on the situations on the tape. Use what you remember about the facts and details to answer them.

1. How do you think Darrell feels about hearing Mr. John's boxing stories?

2. What does Darrell say that gives you this impression?

3. What does Mr. John infer about the picture in the newspaper?

4. What details in the picture help Mr. John figure out what happened?

5. Why does Darrell bring Mr. John the article about burglar-proofing your home?

6. How do you think Mr. John feels about hearing what Darrell has to say?

7. What does Mr. John say and do to give you this impression?

8. Based on what Candy and Rhonda say, what can you infer about the price of Cadillacs and Continentals?

9. Based on the information in the car ad, what kind of shape do you think the car's body is in?

10. How do you think Candy feels at first about Rhonda's eagerness to buy the car mentioned in the ad?

11. What does Candy say to give you this impression?

Check your answers on page 41

In the last program, you saw that important information may not be directly stated in a reading passage. To find this information, you must look carefully at the facts and details in the passage. Here's an example:

> At one time, only rich people could afford home burglar alarms, and professionals were needed to install them. Today, it is possible to buy a do-it-yourself alarm system for less than $100—a mere fraction of the cost of the professionally installed systems. These alarms work by sounding a loud noise when they sense that a burglar is present. The sound is so loud that it will scare away the typical burglar and warn you, your family, and your neighbors of the possible danger.

1. Which of the following can be inferred from the information in the passage?
   (a) Today, burglar alarms do not cost more than $100.
   (b) All burglar alarms must be installed by a professional.
   (c) Some home burglar alarm systems still are expensive.
   (d) Only rich people need burglar alarms.

The first sentence implies that home burglar alarms were once very expensive. The second sentence states that it is now possible to buy a do-it-yourself alarm system for less than $100. From this you can infer that although it is possible to buy a less expensive alarm system, some systems still are expensive. Thus, (c) is the correct inference.

2. Based on the information in the passage, you can infer that
   (a) burglar alarms do not benefit your neighbors
   (b) a burglar alarm is not a guarantee that your home will never be robbed
   (c) a burglar alarm is not loud enough to awaken a person who is asleep
   (d) burglar alarms can go off accidentally

The last sentence of the passage states that the alarm will scare away the typical burglar. This means that not every burglar will be scared away. From this you can infer that a burglar alarm is no guarantee that your home will never be robbed. Thus, (b) is the correct inference.

Remember, whenever you make an inference, you are guessing something that is not directly stated in the passage. The more evidence you find that supports the inference, the surer you can be that your inference is correct.

Read the next passages. Then answer the questions that follow each passage.

Passage 1

Burglar alarms fall into two categories: perimeter systems and ultrasonic systems.

Perimeter systems: Perimeter systems set up an alarm "boundary" in your home. Small switches, called sensors, are installed on the doors and windows. Special sensors are available for under carpets, rugs, and stairtread coverings. If someone opens a window or steps on the carpet, the sensor is disturbed, and the sensor sends out a signal to the system's control box, which sounds the alarm. Sensors usually are connected to the control box by wire, although some sensors come equipped with a transmitter that sends a signal to a receiver in the control box.

Ultrasonic systems: In ultrasonic systems, the transmitter and receiver are in the same box. The transmitter sends out a constant signal that covers a cone-shaped area of your home. Any movement within that area sets off the alarm.

1. According to the passage, burglar alarms fall into what two categories?

2. Based on the information in the passage, you can infer that in the perimeter system
   (a) the sensors used probably are made of plastic
   (b) the sensors used under rugs are different from the sensors used in windows
   (c) each sensor takes only a few minutes to install
   (d) your home is fully protected even if you do not have a sensor in every window and door

3. What evidence in the passage supports the above inference?

4. Which of the following statements can be inferred from the information in the passage?
   (a) The perimeter system is more expensive than the ultrasonic system.
   (b) The ultrasonic system is more popular than the perimeter system.
   (c) Sensors do not work unless they are wired to the control box.
   (d) Sensors are not used in the ultrasonic system.

5. What evidence in the passage supports the above inference?

6. Based on the information in the passage, which of the two systems can you infer requires the most installation work?

Check your answers on page 41

Passage 2

NEXT MONTH YOU COULD BE 30 LBS. LIGHTER.

- **LOSE UP TO A POUND A DAY**
  The Slim Down system will help you lose up to a pound a day without drugs or injections, without strenuous exercise, without even being hungry!
- **NO DECISIONS, NO MISTAKES**
  Instead of counting calories, you'll eat delicious, pre-packaged Slim Down meals. You don't have to make food decisions so you can't make a mistake . . . all you do is enjoy eating again while you lose!
- **LOSE THAT WEIGHT FOR GOOD**
  After you've lost the weight, we'll show you how to keep it off for good . . . you'll learn all the secrets every thin person knows!

CALL TODAY FOR A FREE, NO OBLIGATION WEIGHT ANALYSIS

WEIGHT LOSS SUCCESS CERTIFICATE

If you don't lose your unwanted weight, you could get $1,000!

Only Slim Down could make this amazing offer you must lose the weight you want to lose on our program or you get $1,000 (in accordance with terms of Weight Loss Success Certificate backed by the World Famous London Insurer). You'll receive an actual Certificate when you enroll . . . and you will reach your goal or $1,000 is yours!

Over 350 Centers Nationwide

slim down
weight loss centers

Call today for a free, no obligation consultation.

680-8600

1. According to the passage, how much money can you receive if you do not lose the weight you want to lose?

2. According to the passage, who backs the "Weight Loss Success Certificate"?

3. Based on the information in the passage, you can infer that
   (a) the company accepts credit cards
   (b) the weight loss program costs $1,000
   (c) the weight loss program is free
   (d) the company will only accept cash

4. What evidence in the passage supports the above inference?

5. Which of the following statements can be inferred from the information in the passage?
   (a) The "Weight Loss Success Certificate" shown on the ad guarantees you $1,000 if you do not lose your unwanted weight.
   (b) Not everyone who doesn't lose their unwanted weight will receive $1,000.
   (c) The $1,000 offer is not available outside the United States.
   (d) Some people have already collected $1,000 from the company.

6. What evidence in the passage supports the above inference?

Check your answers on page 42

Passage 3

Your automatic drip coffeemaker needs help!
Here comes Drip Clean!

Did you know that your automatic drip coffeemaker collects mineral deposits from the water that passes through it? And did you know that because of this, it takes longer to make hot, delicious coffee? And that's not all. These mineral deposits eventually can cause your automatic drip coffeemaker to break down.

Never fear. Here comes Drip Clean. Drip Clean completely removes mineral buildup. So you don't have to wait so long for your coffee. And your machine won't break down because of mineral buildup.

Drip Clean has no offensive odor, and it's cheaper than leading vinegars.

So save your automatic drip coffeemaker. Buy Drip Clean.

1. Which of the following can be inferred from the information in the passage?
   (a) Drip Clean can be used to clean any coffee pot.
   (b) Drip Clean is made with vinegar.
   (c) Vinegar is sometimes used to clean automatic drip coffeemakers.
   (d) Vinegar can leave mineral deposits in your automatic drip coffeemaker.

2. What evidence in the passage supports the above inference?

3. Based on the information in the passage, you can infer that
   (a) water contains minerals.
   (b) your automatic drip coffeemaker will never break down if you use Drip Clean.
   (c) you must use Drip Clean after each time you make coffee.
   (d) Drip Clean makes coffee taste better.

4. What evidence in the passage supports the above inference?

Check your answers on page 42

Watch Part 2: *"The Inside Story"*

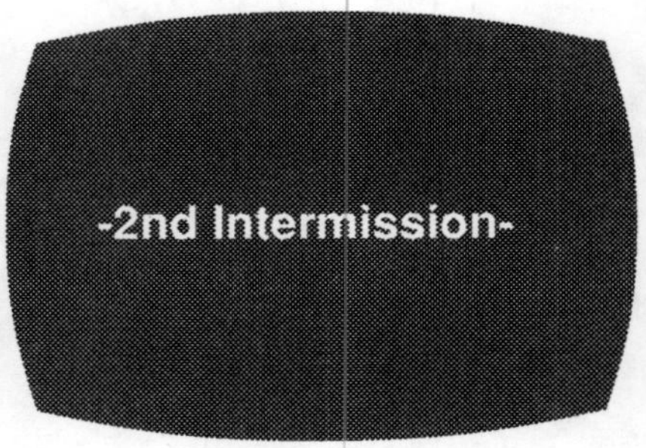

You have seen that a writer does not always directly state what he wants to communicate to you. To find this unstated information, you must make inferences.

An inference is a guess based on the facts and details in a reading passage and on your own common sense. You have already seen how to find an unstated main idea and how to draw logical conclusions. These are two types of inferences.

When you make an inference, you discover information that is not directly stated, but implied. Here's a simple example:

> The sun beat down on this warm summer day. George waited at the corner for the light to change. He took out his handkerchief and wiped his forehead.

What does the writer expect you to infer? For one thing, when he uses the word "light," he expects you to know he is talking about a traffic light. In order to make the inference, you first must look for facts and details in the passage—*waiting on the corner* for the light to *change*. By using your common sense—you know that at many *street corners* there are traffic lights and that traffic lights *change*—you can infer that the word "light" refers to a traffic light.

What else can you infer about the passage? The writer expects you to infer that George is perspiring. In order to make this inference, you first must look for facts and details in the passage—*sun beating down, warm summer day, wiping his forehead.* And by using your common sense—you know that on sunny, warm summer days people often perspire and that on such a day, when people wipe their foreheads, they usually do it to wipe off perspiration—you can infer that George is perspiring.

There are many types of inferences you can make about a passage. Inferences can:

- add to the facts and details in the passage
  (You inferred that "light" meant "traffic light.")
- make general conclusions about people or situations in the passage (you practiced this skill in the previous unit)
  (You inferred, or concluded, that George wiped his forehead because he was perspiring.)
- explain why something happens
  (You inferred that the traffic jam was caused by an accident.)
- explain what will happen if a certain action is taken
  (You inferred that if the drivers of the cars didn't pay attention to what they were doing, the cars would collide.)
- describe the writer's opinions or feelings about his topic
  (A writer often will not directly state how he feels about his topic. But you sometimes can infer how he feels by studying the way he says things.)

Also, remember that an inference is a guess. In order to make a correct inference, or guess, it is important to get as many clues as you can from the facts and details in the passage.

Now read the following passage:

> What does $475 mean to you? A paycheck? A vacation? To a burglar, it's the average value of a single haul—the TV, stereo, or tools he steals.
>
> It doesn't take much to outsmart most burglars. They're usually not "pros." Most often they're kids taking advantage of an easy mark. So easy, in fact, that often they can go right in through an unlocked door or window. No wonder there's a burglary every ten seconds!

From these two paragraphs you can infer:

(1) Many burglaries occur because people don't protect their property.

The facts and details in the passage state that burglars often can get into a home through an unlocked door or window. From this you can infer that many burglaries occur because people don't do the things—like locking doors and windows—that will help them protect their property. In this example, the inference is a general conclusion.

(2) If you lock your doors and windows, you reduce the chance of your home being burglarized.

The facts and details say that some homes are burglarized because the doors and windows are unlocked. What will happen if you do lock your doors and windows? You can infer that locking the doors and windows is a simple way to reduce the chances of your home being burglarized. In this example, the inference explains what will happen if a certain action is taken.

Based on the information in the passage, can you make the following inference?

(3) Your home will not be burglarized if you lock your doors and windows.

Is there anything in the passage that suggests, or implies, that locking your doors will guarantee that your home will not be burglarized? No. All you can infer is that locking your doors and windows will help prevent burglaries. There is not enough evidence in the passage to allow you to make this inference.

Now read the following passage:

Want to stop the clock on burglars? A good first step is to lock your doors, *always*—even when you're going out "for just a minute." Remember these simple tips, too:

- Check your locks—they should be the "dead bolt" type with a strong metal bar extending one inch into the door frame.
- Too hot to close and lock windows? Put nails in the window frames so the windows can't be opened more than a few inches until you take the nails out.
- Try this simple safeguard for sliding glass doors: When you close and lock the door, put a small wooden beam or broom handle in the door track. Even if the lock is jimmied, the door will be hard to open.
- Taking a trip? Make sure your home always looks "lived-in," especially when you're not there.
  - — Stop newspaper and mail delivery, or ask a neighbor to collect them so things won't pile up outside your door.
  - — Use automatic timers to turn lights and radios on and off. You can buy timers at hardware or department stores for under $10. Set them so lights go on in different rooms at different times.
- Mark things you own that burglars like—TV, stereo, CB radios, or tools—with a personal identification number, which is something they don't like. Announce the fact by sticking a warning sign on your door or window. The police can help you mark things and give you the warning sticker. Just ask about **Operation Identification.**

Which of the following inferences can be made about the passage?

(1) Sliding glass doors usually do not have locks.

(2) A burglar usually will not break into a house if he thinks someone is home.

(3) Dead bolt-type locks are the best type of lock for preventing burglaries.
(4) A burglar will never steal an item that has a personal identification number.
(5) Operation Identification is a program in which police help citizens give their valuables identification numbers.

Look at the choices one at a time:

(1) Sliding glass doors usually do not have locks.

Does anything in the sliding glass door section tell you that these doors do not have locks? No. In fact, a part of that section reads: "… when you close and *lock* the door …" This implies that sliding doors do have locks. Choice (1) cannot be inferred from the information in the passage.

(2) A burglar usually will not break into a house if he thinks someone is home.

The fourth section of the passage states that it is important for your home to look lived-in. Since the passage mainly talks about preventing burglaries, this implies that making your home look lived-in is one way to prevent burglaries. From this you can infer that a burglar usually will not break into a house if he thinks someone is home. Thus, (2) can be inferred from the information in the passage.

(3) Dead bolt-type locks are the best locks for preventing burglaries.

The first section of the passage emphasizes that your locks should be dead bolt-type locks. Since the passage mainly talks about preventing burglaries, this implies that dead bolt-type locks help prevent burglaries. Since this is the only type of lock that the passage recommends, you can infer that dead bolt-type locks are the best locks for preventing burglaries. Thus, (3) can be inferred from the information in the passage.

(4) A burglar will never steal an item that has a personal identification number.

The last section of the passage states that you should mark your valuables with personal identification numbers. Since the passage mainly talks about preventing burglaries, you can say that marking your valuables with personal identification numbers will help prevent burglaries. But does this mean that a burglar will never steal an item with a personal identification number? No. There is not enough evidence in the passage to support this inference. Thus, (4) cannot be inferred from the information in the passage.

(5) Operation Identification is a program in which police help citizens give their valuables identification numbers.

The last section of the passage tells you to ask about Operation Identification. You can guess that this sentence refers to the sentence that directly precedes it: *The police can help you mark your things and give you the warning sticker.* Since this section of the passage talks about personal identification numbers, you can assume that *mark your things* means to give them personal identification numbers. From this information, you can infer that when you ask about Operation Identification, you are asking about a program in which the police help citizens give their valuables personal identification numbers. Thus, (5) can be inferred from the information in the passage.

From these examples, you can see that the writer of a reading passage does not always directly state what he wants to communicate to you. Instead, he suggests, or implies, information about his topic. And he expects you to infer this important information from the facts and details in the passage. By carefully looking at the facts and details and by using your common sense, you will be able to figure out what the writer didn't directly say.

Read the following passages. Then answer the questions that follow each one.

Passage 4

A right of entry or access is a legal term that means you have given the landlord advance permission to enter your dwelling. This right is for the purpose of making repairs or improvements or providing agreed-upon services. The landlord may also need entry to show the unit to prospective purchasers, lenders, tenants, workmen, or contractors. The landlord should come at reasonable hours and at your convenience, except in an emergency. Your lease may limit or expand this right, so check it before signing.

1. According to the passage, to whom may the landlord need to show your dwelling?

2. Which of the following is the main idea of the passage?
   (a) Your landlord is allowed to enter your dwelling only if there is an emergency.
   (b) Right of entry or access allows your landlord to enter your dwelling in certain situations.
   (c) Your landlord can gain access to your dwelling only if he comes at your convenience.
   (d) There is a clause in your lease that describes right of entry or access.

3. Which of the following can be inferred from the passage?
   (a) Your landlord must ask your permission before he enters your dwelling in an emergency.
   (b) Your landlord is not allowed to have a key to your dwelling.
   (c) Your landlord will always give you advance notice before he enters your dwelling.
   (d) Your landlord can enter your dwelling at any time if there is an emergency.

4. The passage implies that
   (a) right of entry applies only if your dwelling is an apartment
   (b) the right-of-entry clause is the same in all leases
   (c) right of entry takes effect when you sign your lease
   (d) if you feel that your landlord has abused his right of entry, you can take him to court

Check your answers on page 43

Passage 5

What Creditors Look For

The Three C's. Creditors look for an ability to repay a debt and a willingness to do so—and sometimes for a little extra security to protect their loans. They speak of the three C's of credit: capacity, character, and collateral.

Capacity. Can you repay the debt? Creditors ask for employment information: your occupation, how long you've worked, how much you earn. They also want to know your expenses: how many dependents you have or whether you pay alimony or child support.

Character: Will you repay the debt? Creditors will look at your credit history: how much you owe, how often you borrow, whether you pay bills on time, and whether you live within your means. They also look for signs of stability: how long you've lived at your present address, whether you own or rent, and whether you are insured.

Collateral: Is the creditor fully protected if you fail to repay? Creditors want to know what you may have that could be used to secure your loan and what sources you have for repaying debt other than income, such as savings, investments, or property.

1. According to the passage, what signs of stability do creditors look for?

2. According to the passage, what sources other than income can be used to repay your loan?

3. Which sentence is the main idea sentence of the passage?

4. Which of the following can be inferred from the information in the passage?
   (a) The creditor will ask for a copy of your income tax return.
   (b) The creditor will not give you a loan if you pay alimony.
   (c) The creditor probably will not give you a loan if you have no dependents.
   (d) The creditor probably will not give you a loan if you are unemployed.

5. The passage implies that
   (a) a person who moves frequently may have a hard time getting a loan
   (b) it is easier to get a loan if you have taken out loans before
   (c) creditors would rather give a loan to a person who rents a house
   (d) you must pay off all of your other debts before you can get a loan

6. From the information in the passage, you can infer that
   (a) if you do not repay your loan, the creditor can take all of your property
   (b) it is easier to get a loan if you have other sources besides income for repaying the loan
   (c) creditors will not give you a loan unless you have a savings account
   (d) creditors would rather give a loan to a person who has no investments

Check your answers on page 43

Passage 6

To "poison-proof" your home …

1. Keep household products and medicines out of reach and out of sight of children, preferably in a locked cabinet or closet. Even if you must leave the room for only an instant, remove the container to a safe spot.
2. Store medicines separately from other household products and keep these items in their original containers—never in cups or soft-drink bottles.
3. Be sure all products are properly labeled, and read the label before using.
4. Always turn the light on when giving or taking medicine.
5. Since children tend to imitate adults, avoid taking medications in their presence.
6. Refer to medicines by their proper names. They are not candies.
7. Clean out your medicine cabinet periodically. Get rid of old medicines by flushing them down the drain, rinsing out the container in water, and then discarding the container.

8. Ask for and use household substances that are available in child-resistant packaging. Insist on safety packaging for prescription medicines. Resecure safety features carefully after using. Safety packaging gives extra protection to your children.

1. According to the passage, where are the best places to store household products and medicines?

2. According to the passage, what procedure should you use to discard old medicines?

3. Based on the information in the passage, which of the following conclusions is logical?
   (a) Children should not have access to household products and medicines.
   (b) Children should never take medicine.
   (c) Children's medicine does not come in child-resistant packaging.
   (d) Children should never take medicine that is made for adults.

4. The passage implies that
   (a) more children die from poisoning than from any other cause of death
   (b) household products are safer than medicines to have around the house
   (c) some children eat and drink medicine because they think it is candy
   (d) non-prescription medicines do not come in child-resistant packaging

Check your answers on page 44

Watch Part 3

In this program, you have seen that a writer does not always directly state important ideas. Instead, he may imply, or suggest, these ideas. In order to find this unstated information, you must make inferences. You have seen that by looking carefully at the facts and details and by using your common sense, you can guess, or infer, ideas that are not directly stated in the passage.

Vocabulary Review

The following vocabulary exercise is based on the vocabulary words at the beginning of this lesson. For each sentence, choose the correct word from the list below and write that word in the space provided. (Each word is used only once.)

additives	humidity	ransacked
artificial	illusion	repel
burglary	infection	stabilizers
defy	infer	strike plate
guarantee	neutralizing	symbol
humidifier	obsolete	

1. __________ are additives that help improve and maintain the quality of food.

2. When you read a passage, you look for facts and details and use your common sense to __________ information that is not directly stated in the passage.

3. There have been so many break-ins in this city lately that the police have formed an anti-__________ patrol.

4. Sharon is going to buy a __________ because the heat in her apartment dries out her sinuses.

5. The written __________ that came with the blender says the blender will run for a year without breaking down.

6. Just as the Maple Leaf stands for the nation of Canada, the American flag is the __________ of the United States.

7. Debby does not buy foods that contain stabilizers or other artificial __________; she buys only all-natural foods.

8. Last night, Doris returned to any empty home; her apartment had been __________.

9. Skunks use their offensive scent to __________ potential enemies.

10. __________ lakes are not formed by nature; they are created by man.

11. When Bob goes out, he leaves the lights on to create the __________ that he is home.

12. A __________ substance can be used to take away the bad effects of a chemical.

13. If germs get into a wound, an __________ usually will develop.

14. Sarah did not __________ the orders of her supervisor; she simply questioned them.

15. Some people don't mind the dry heat of the desert; they say the low __________ makes the air comfortable.

16. Some people believed that push-button telephones would make dial telephones __________.

17. When the burglar kicked in the door, the __________ flew right off the door frame.

Check your answers on page 44

Reading Skills Review

Passage 7

Lights On Emergency Vehicles

RED LIGHT: Means an ambulance, police car, or fire apparatus. Upon their approach, the law says that all vehicles must get as far to the right-hand side of the road as possible and STOP.
BLUE LIGHT: May mean a police car or an active member of a volunteer fire department or company who is on his way to the scene of a fire or other emergency. The right of way should be granted this vehicle.
WHITE LIGHT: Flashing or revolving means fire emergency apparatus or vehicles of executive officers responding to an emergency; should be granted the right of way.

1. According to the passage, what types of emergency vehicles have red lights?

2. According to the passage, what must you do when a vehicle with a red light approaches?

3. Which of the following can be inferred from the information in the passage?
   (a) The right of way should not be granted to a vehicle with a red light.
   (b) You are not required by law to get to the right and stop for a vehicle with a blue light.
   (c) There are more vehicles on the road with a white light than there are vehicles with a red or blue light.
   (d) White lights on emergency vehicles are the only lights that flash or revolve.

Check your answers on page 45

Passage 8

Legal Aid and Legal Services

WHAT THEY ARE:

Legal Aid and Legal Services offices help people who cannot afford to hire private lawyers and who meet financial eligibility requirements. There are more than 1,000 of these offices around the country, staffed by lawyers, paralegals (people who have taken courses in legal assistance), and law students. All offer free legal services to those who qualify.

In some cities, both Legal Aid and Legal Services offices are federally funded. Legal Aid offices may also be financed by state, local, or private funding, or by local bar associations. The Legal Services Corporation, located in Washington, D.C., is funded by the federal government; it, in turn, awards grants to local Legal Services programs around the country.

Also, many law schools throughout the nation conduct law clinics, where students assist Legal Aid and other lawyers as part of their training.

WHAT THEY DO:

These offices give legal assistance with problems involving landlord-tenant disputes; credit; utilities; and family issues, such as divorce and adoption. They also work on cases involving social security, welfare, unemployment, and workers' compensation.

1. According to the passage, from what sources may Legal Aid offices get the funds they need?

2. In your own words, state the main idea of the passage.

3. Which sentence is the main idea sentence?

4. Based on the information in the passage, which of the following do you think would NOT be handled by Legal Aid or Legal Services?
   (a) A landlord threatens to evict a tenant.
   (b) A laid-off worker is refused unemployment insurance.
   (c) A man is arrested and charged with assault.
   (d) A woman claims that she was unfairly refused a loan.

5. Which of the following can be inferred from the information in the passage?
   (a) If you go to Legal Aid or Legal Services, a law student will take your case.
   (b) Private lawyers are better qualified than Legal Aid and Legal Services lawyers.
   (c) Legal Aid or Legal Services will not take your case if you cannot afford a private lawyer.
   (d) Before Legal Aid or Legal Services will take your case, they probably will want to know how much money you make.

6. Which of the following can be inferred from the information in the passage?
   (a) Legal Aid is made up of individual offices and probably has no central corporation.
   (b) The federal government is running out of money to finance Legal Aid.
   (c) Legal Services lawyers are not as qualified as Legal Aid lawyers.
   (d) Local bar associations help finance the Legal Services Corporation.

Check your answers on page 46

Passage 9

As a consumer, buy wisely. When prices are skyrocketing, don't buy things you don't need just because you think the price will rise even more. If you don't think you can afford something, don't buy it.

Shop carefully. Compare prices and use unit pricing where it is available. Keep an eye out for specials and sales. And don't be afraid to ask why prices are going up if you think an increase is excessive or unjustified. And remember, when some products are in short supply—like gasoline or other energy products—the best way to save money is to use less; conserve. Every gallon of oil saved through conservation helps fight inflation.

Budget wisely. Live within your means—don't take on more personal debt than you can handle. Living within our means applies to government, business, and families as well. And if you possibly can, try to save some of your income.

1. According to the passage, what should you do if you don't think you can afford a product?

2. What products does the passage mention as examples of products that are in short supply?

3. In your own words, state the main idea of the passage.

4. Which of the following can be inferred from the information in the passage?
   (a) Saving some of your income is not easy.
   (b) If you think a price increase in unjustified, the store will lower the price.
   (c) Inflation is going to get worse in the years to come.
   (d) You should spend your money now because products will be more expensive in the future.

5. When the wrtier says that you should "live within your means," you can infer that he means
   (a) you should spend your money now
   (b) you should use credit cards when you go shopping
   (c) you should not spend more money than you make
   (d) you should make contributions to government

Check your answers on page 46

Passage 10

Protect Yourself Against Fraud

Compared to burglars or robbers, con artists have it made. They don't need tools or guns. They rely on tall tales and smooth talking. They may be young or old, men or women—"nice" people, the kind you run into every day. But they make their living convincing you to hand over your cash for products or services they'll never deliver.

There are countless ways to fool people into giving their money away. Often victims don't know what happened—at least not right away.

You may not know what fraud is either. If you learn to recognize it, you won't fall for it. Here are some simple signs that should serve as a "fraud alarm":

- Somebody offers you something for nothing? You can bet you're going to get nothing for something.
- The deal is "too good to be true"? If that's the case, it probably isn't true. Merchandise that's incredibly cheap, offers of an "amazing investment opportunity," or "deals" on home repairs usually are no bargain.
- You're asked to provide large sums in cash? Watch out! Here are some typical tricks: They want "good faith" money. They ask you to withdraw your savings in cash so the bank examiner can catch a dishonest employee. They insist on cash payment before delivering your purchase. Don't be fooled. If you hand over your cash, that's the last you'll see of it—and the crooks.
- Lots of pressure to sign a contract? They might not want you to notice something. Wait a while and read it over carefully. Take it to a lawyer. Or ask your Better Business Bureau if the seller is on the level.
- If you sign a contract but later you have second thoughts, don't be afraid to call it off! In most states the law gives you three days to change your mind.

1. According to the passage, what usually happens when you accept someone's offer of something for nothing?

2. According to the passage, what should you do if someone pressures you to sign a contract?

3. Based on the information in the passage, which of the following conclusions is logical?
   (a) A contract can be called off only if you can prove that the seller is trying to con you.
   (b) Once a contract is signed, you cannot get out of it.
   (c) You cannot call off a contract two weeks after you sign it.
   (d) You must sign a contract within three days from the day you are requested to sign it.

4. The passage implies that
   (a) people who are not familiar with con artists' tricks are the most likely victims of fraud
   (b) the police have no power to stop con artists
   (c) fraud is more common in big cities than it is in rural areas
   (d) women are more likely than men to be victims of con artists' tricks

5. Which of the following can be inferred from the information in the passage?
   (a) Con artists are nice people.
   (b) Con artists never carry weapons.
   (c) You cannot tell a con artist by the way he looks.
   (d) You may not know it, but you run into con artists every day.

6. The passage implies that
   (a) a contract should never be signed before the Better Businesss Bureau has seen it
   (b) sellers who use contracts are not on the level
   (c) a contract can be written in such a way that the person who signs it will lose money
   (d) you should read a contract only if you feel that there is a possibility of fraud

Check your answers on page 47.

Passage 11

Cast Your Vote for

☒**CREATION**

OR

☒**EVOLUTION**

Where do you stand in this vital debate?

1. Do you agree with the "theories" of evolution that DENY the Biblical account of creation?

☐ YES ☐ NO

2. Do you agree that public school teachers should be permitted to teach our children as fact that they descended from APES?

☐ YES ☐ NO

3. Do you agree with the evolutionists who are attempting to PREVENT the Biblical account of creation from also being taught in public schools?

☐ YES ☐ NO

Answer and return today—
Your vote urgently needed!

In return for your vote, I'll send you a FREE copy of "IN THE BEGINNING"—a 111- page book that gives overwhelming evidence in favor of creation.

Gospel Time
Fallsburg, Al 21717

Name__________
Address__________
City__________
State __________ Zip__________

Any contribution to this campaign
is tax deductable and deeply appreciated!
Please return this Entire Ballot

1. Do you think the writer agrees with the theories of evolution that deny the Biblical account of creation?

2. What evidence in the passage helped you answer the above question?

3. Do you think the writer agrees that public school teachers should be permitted to teach our children as fact that they descended from apes?

4. What evidence in the passage helped you answer the above question?

5. Do you think the writer agrees with the evolutionists who are attempting to prevent the Biblical account of creation from also being taught in public schools?

6. What evidence in the passage helped you answer the above question?

Check your answers on page 47

TV Scripts—"More Pages"

ACT I
"Gray Panther Attack"

Fade in on Darrell entering Mr. John's shop; he finds John on the phone, engaged in a heated conversation with someone.

MR. JOHN *(on phone)*: That's right, Everett! We'll make 'em sit up and take notice. They'll know it when the Gray Panthers attack! ... All right, I'll see you about 5 o'clock—right in the middle of rush hour. And Everett, don't forget your cane or umbrella. Okay, see you later.

He hangs up the phone.

DARRELL: A gray panther attack?? What's that? What's goin' on? This got anything to do with the *Black* Panthers?

MR. J: No, huh-uh. We're not quite as militant as the Black Panthers—probably because we're a little bit older. For your information, the Gray Panthers is a group of senior citizens who want to make sure that all you children under 60 don't neglect your elders.

DARRELL: Have I been neglecting you, Mr. J?

MR. J: It's not you, Darrell. It's the government. The federal government and the local government.

Picks up paper.

MR. J: Listen to this article: "People living on fixed incomes, like the elderly, are the hardest hit by inflation. As prices for necessary items like housing, food, clothing, heat, and electricity continue to skyrocket, people on fixed incomes are forced to do without. If heating bills rise to expected levels this winter, some retired people may actually have to choose between heat and food." Now ain't that great! Do we freeze to death or starve to death? And listen to this other article: "Congress is in a tax-cutting mood. It is expected that the lawmakers will kill programs that provide financial assistance to help the needy and the elderly with their winter fuel bills. At the same time, it is expected that the defense budget will be greatly increased." Now what do you infer from that?

DARRELL: What do I *what*?

MR. J: *Infer*—what do you make of it, son; what do you get out of it?

DARRELL: Oh yeah, I dig—what's it telling me. Is that what you mean? … I don't know. What's it telling you?

MR. J: It's telling me that the government cares more about buying guns and bombs than it does about taking care of our old people. The same sort of thing is happening on the local level. You know how dangerous it is out here on Jackson Avenue, with all the traffic rushing by, and all the old people in the project have to cross it to get to the market and the laundry and so on. We've tried for years to get the city to put in a crosswalk and a light. It's too expensive, they say. Well, old Josh Cobb got hit by a delivery truck yesterday afternoon. Put him in the hospital with a broken hip. We told 'em it would happen. But we're gonna make sure it doesn't happen again!

DARRELL: Hmmm, I can infer from what you say that that's where the Gray Panther attack comes in.

MR. J: You got it.

DARRELL: So what are you gonna do, take over city hall?

MR. J: Just be over here at Jackson and Third at 5 this evening and you'll see some action!

Dissolve to street corner scene. Cars are backed up in both directions; horns are blowing; cops are out in force; so are the news cameras. Camera pans long line of frustrated motorists; finally we see the reason: A line of Gray Panthers, including Mr. John, is blocking the street by holding onto each other's canes and umbrellas.

Two cops are conferring; one is talking by police radio with the mayor.

COP: We can't arrest all these old people with all the TV cameras around; it wouldn't look too good. They say they won't move until you come down here. Something about a crosswalk and traffic light ... Okay, I'll tell 'em.

He goes over near the line of old people.

COP: All right! The mayor's on his way. Now, will you please move out of the street?

The Gray Panthers cheer.

Mr. J catches Darrell's eye; he raises his fist and winks, then shouts to Darrell.

MR. J: I told you they'd have to pay us some mind.

DARRELL: Chalk one up for the Gray Panthers!

Fade out.

ACT II
"Drive, She Said"

Rhonda and Candy pull up outside the bar where Candy works; Rhonda cuts the engine off.

CANDY: Thanks for the ride, Rhonda. What are you gonna do with the rest of your afternoon?

Rhonda picks up a driver's manual.

RHONDA: Well, I'm gonna look over this book once more, then I'm gonna go down and take the test to get a driver's license.

CANDY: A driver's license! Great! It's a good thing to have! Rhonda—you mean to tell me you've been driving around for the last few days without a license?

RHONDA: Well, I tried to get one a few years ago, but I was in Ronald's big old truck and my foot slipped off the brake and hit the gas.... I ran into the back of the police car of the officer who was giving me the test.

CANDY: So you flunked it, huh?

RHONDA: Yeah. And I'm kinda afraid I'll do something else just as dumb. But I've fixed my hair special, so at least I'll look better.

CANDY: Good luck. ... Do you know all the stuff in here?

She points to the book.

RHONDA: Pretty well. I want to go over the road signs and hand signals. They're sort of interesting, you know. It's like the pictures on the signs tell little stories and we have to figure them out. Look at this one. What's he doing?

Close-up of pedestrian/crosswalk sign (man walking).

CANDY: Looks to me like he's doing the Funky Chicken, or the Georgia Strut!

RHONDA: No, silly. He's walking across the street. It means there's a crosswalk and you better slow down. He does look kind of funny, though.... All right now, do you know what it means when I do this?

Rhonda puts her arm out the window, pointing downward.

CANDY: It means you want to get a suntan on your arm.

RHONDA: Close! It means I'm slowing down and stopping. It's so the person behind me won't run into me.

CANDY: Hey! Do you know what that means?

Candy leans out the window and waves her arms; she puts her fingers to her mouth and lets out a whistle.

RHONDA: I can't imagine.

CANDY: It means "woman seeks handsome man on street corner!"

RHONDA: And what if the wrong man tries to take you up on it?

CANDY: There's a sign for that, too.

RHONDA: Candy! Stop—someone will see!

CANDY: All right, all right. Say, what's it got in there about drunk drivers? I'd like to be able to tell it to the creeps that come in the bar.

RHONDA: Let's see ... It says that alcohol is responsible for about half of all car wrecks, and it's the single most important human factor connected with highway deaths. Hmm, they give you a test to find out how much alcohol is in your blood. If you have too much they take your license away. And listen to this: "The only thing that will lessen the effects of alcohol or sober a person up is time. Such things as coffee or a cold shower do not work. So no alcohol should be consumed before driving, since even small amounts impair driving ability."

CANDY: Shoot, if they cracked down on that there'd be a lot of people walking home from this joint every night! ... Well, it's just about 4; I better go on in. See you tomorrow.

Candy gets out.

RHONDA: Okay, Candy. Wish me luck.

CANDY: Good luck.

Dissolve to Rhonda standing with a policeman next to her car; she just finished the test.

POLICEMAN: Okay, Miss. Here's your temporary license. They'll mail you the permanent one. ... You know, I'd swear I've seen you somewhere before.

RHONDA: Nope, I don't think so, officer. I have to get going and pick up my little girl. Thanks for giving me the test.

She gets in the car and starts it; he leans in the passenger window.

POLICEMAN: I'd swear I've seen you somewhere, I just can't remember where. Hey, didn't somebody drive you over here?

RHONDA: Uh, no.

POLICEMAN: But you didn't have a license!

RHONDA: Well, I do now! Bye-bye.

She drives off, leaving him confused.

Fade out.

ACT III
"Doughnuts and Dunk Shots"

It's Sunday morning; Mr. John is sitting in his easy chair; the Sunday paper is spread all around. He's eating a doughnut, drinking coffee, and watching a talk show on TV. He hears a knock, gets up and goes into the shop, sees Darrell at the door, and lets him in.

MR. JOHN: Good morning, Darrell.

DARRELL: Hey, Mr. John, how you doin'? I just came by to see if you needed anything.

They pass back through the shop into Mr. John's living quarters.

MR. J: Naw, I don't need anything but a day like today, when I can sit around and do nothing. "Lay down and rest from your labors," and all that. Come on in here and help me eat these doughnuts. What's happening with you today?

Darrell starts with two doughnuts; he and Mr. J sit down.

DARRELL: Not much. I'm headed over to the playground to shoot a little hoop. You know how it goes: Saturday night you put your moves on the women and Sunday afternoon you put your moves on the dudes on the courts.

MR. J: Both of those are young men's games. I've been putting my moves on the Sunday paper. And I watched a couple of Sunday morning talk shows; they can be pretty interesting sometimes. The TV stations are requiared to put on a few public service programs—programs that are helpful, that give out information—or the government gets on their case for not doing anything for the public. So the stations put 'em on Sunday morning, when hardly anyone is watching. But you can learn about some pretty important stuff…

DARRELL: What kind of stuff?

MR. J: Well, it's interesting that you're headed for the playground, because the most interesting thing I saw this morning was a black man talking about a myth that most young blacks embrace.

DARRELL: What do you mean?

MR. J: What's the quickest, surest way for a young black kid to get out of the ghetto and make big money?

DARRELL: Make it in the pros, I guess. You get real good and become a professional athlete with a big contract.

MR. J: That's right. But this man, Harry Edwards, says that's a myth and that it's unfortunate that most black youngsters believe it.

DARRELL: Wait a minute, Mr. John. What's a myth, anyway? And who's this guy, Harry Edwards?

MR. J: A myth can be a story that's been handed down from ancient times, like stories about Egyptian or Greek gods: Apollo pulls the sun through the sky with his chariot—that sort of thing. But a myth can also be a lie or a falsehood. That's another definition of a myth. It can be an idea that gets put over on people. Sometimes people will perpetuate, or keep alive, a myth so they can keep things from changing. The slave-owners, for instance—they tried to perpetuate the myth that blacks are inferior, so they could brutalize millions of our ancestors and keep them in bondage. This man Edwards is a college professor who has studied black athletes to see how society treats them. He said it's a myth that the shortest road from the ghetto to success is through sports. Sure, we read about the players who sign the big contracts, but you don't hear about the million others who try it but don't make it. Edwards said there are less than 1,000 blacks making their living as professional athletes. He cited some interesting figures and I scribbled 'em down, just so I could tell you all about it.

John looks for a certain section of the paper and finds it. The newspaper has some numbers scribbled in the margins.

MR. J: Here, the man said almost 700,000 kids play high school basketball, and then the number drops to 15,000 playing college ball. About 4,000 finish their college careers each year, and out of those, only about 200 get drafted by the pros. Out of that 200, only about 50 sign pro contracts. That ain't very many, when you think that millions of black kids see it as their main chance for success. Edwards said instead of a stairway to wealth and stardom, the sports route is a treadmill, or a dead end, for a lot of young blacks. I agree with the man. Our youngsters have to stop concentrating on athletic skills and work on other things.

DARRELL: I hear what he's saying, but if you're good, man, if you can put together some impressive stats, the man's gonna come along and pay you to do your thing.

MR. J: Edwards said the odds against a young athlete making it in the pros are worse than 20,000 to 1. Think about *those* stats. And the odds against you are even worse, because you're black, and because you didn't get through high school. Let's see here...

John looks for another piece of the paper that he scribbled on.

MR. J: ...seventy to eighty percent of the black athletes who make it through high school and get to college never graduate from college. He mentioned the starting five from the 1965 college championship team, the University of Texas at El Paso. All five were black; none of them graduated; none of them made it in the pros. You have to ask yourself, what happened to those guys?

Darrell shrugs and reaches for another doughnut.

Darrell takes a bite or two and then pauses to take in what John is saying.

MR. J: I remember a couple of weeks ago you were moaning about how you wish you hadn't quit high school because it would have made it easier to get to the pros if you played high school and college ball. If you ask me, instead of hitting the boards, you should have been hitting the books. A good education is a lot surer bet than a behind-the-back dribble or a 360-

degree dunk shot.

Darrell dunks his last bite of doughnut in John's coffee and stuffs it in his mouth.

DARRELL: With that dunk 'n' stuff, I've got to get on out of here. I know you're right about an education being more important, Mr. John, and one of these days I'm gonna go one-on-one with the books. But right now I'm gonna go out and "perpetuate a myth"—not 'cause I think that's a good thing to do, but because I just like to play the game.

MR. J: Well, that sounds like a better reason to run around chasing a bunch of people, trying to put a little ball in a hole!

They laugh, fade out.

ACT IV
"To Be or Not To Be ... Obese"

Rhonda and Candy are shopping in the supermarket; they each have a shopping cart that is almost filled. As we fade in on them, they are involved more in a conversation than with shopping; Candy seems upset.

RHONDA: So what are you so upset about? Just because your cousin Lorraine is coming for a few days and wants to stay at your house?

CANDY: Rhonda, my cousin Lorraine IS a house. It makes me really uncomfortable to be around her because she's so fat and she doesn't do anything about it. I've always wanted to tell her to get it together—or un-together, I guess you'd say. I've never understood how she could stand to be so fat. I haven't seen her in over a year, but the last time she was here, she actually got wedged in a doorway in my house! Now my house is little, but getting stuck in a doorway! I mean, *come on!*

RHONDA: She sounds pretty big, all right. But you know, I bet one of the main reasons she makes you uncomfortable is that she reminds you that you could be like that if you didn't watch what you eat. What's that old saying? "There, but for the grace of God, go I," or something like that. In other words, it could be you or me.

They push their carts up to the checkout lines; Rhonda scans the magazines and little booklets; she pulls one of the booklets off the shelf.

RHONDA: … Look, Candy. This little book is called *To Be or Not To Be Obese?* I'm not sure what "obese" means, but it must have to do with being fat, because this drawing on the cover shows a woman going from big and round to slim and curvy. It's only 75 cents. Let's get it for Lorraine. Maybe you can get some ideas on how to help her.

CANDY: All right, but I don't know if she can be helped, at this point.

Rhonda and Candy check out and put their groceries in Rhonda's car.

As they are driving home, Rhonda hands Candy the booklet on obesity.

RHONDA: Here, read a little of this aloud while I'm driving you home. Maybe we'll both learn something.

CANDY: Okay, it says that it's estimated that 40 percent of all Americans are obese, or overweight. "Recent research has shown that more of the blame for being fat lies in metablolic irregularities."

Candy stumbles a little on the words "metabolic irregularities."

CANDY: "In other words, there are significant differences in the way thin people and fat people burn up their calories. Thin people burn up their extra calories, by changing them to heat which radiates out through the skin. Fat people tend to store up their extra calories, instead of burning them"—look, Rhonda, I can see those pork ribs I had for lunch radiating out of my body now!

Candy holds out her arm for Rhonda to see.

Rhonda gives her a skeptical look.

CANDY: "This new research leads us to a more sympathetic understanding of the plight of the overweight person. We can no longer conclude that an obese person simply eats too much or is too lazy to change. This is important to realize, because overweight people need the encouragement and support of family and friends if they are to develop good eating habits and get the right amount of exercise."

RHONDA: They're talking about you, Candy. You have to help Lorraine, instead of just criticizing her. Don't you think?

CANDY: All right, all right. Let me read some more. "'Eat less and move more' is still the best advice. Write down everything you eat for five days and then go through the list to see where you could cut back. Cutting down on sweets, fats, and oils will help, as will eating smaller portions. Also, it's good to cut out second helpings altogether. Another good piece of advice is to eat slowly. It takes the brain about 20 minutes to get the message that you are full. If you wolf your food down in 10 minutes, you may think you're still hungry and eat more. Ten minutes later you feel stuffed. Develop some good exercise habits. Walking briskly for 15 minutes after eating is one good practice. Eventually, you want to build up to 30 minutes of hard exercise at least three times a week. Hard exercise is characterized by increased pulse rate, heavy breathing, and sweating"—hmmm, sounds like love!

Just then they round the corner and Candy's little house comes into view; a woman is standing on the porch.

RHONDA: Who's that on your porch, Candy? Is that your cousin?

CANDY: No, that ain't Lorraine. She'd make the house look tiny. I don't know who that is, but she's no Lorraine, that's for sure.

They pull to a stop and start to get out; suddenly the woman runs up to Candy. She's full-figured, but as Candy said, she's no Lorraine.

WOMAN: Candy! Cousin Candy! It's me, Lorraine.

They embrace; Candy looks like she's seen a ghost.

CANDY: Lorraine, what happened? You look so… I mean, you're not…

LORRAINE: Go ahead, say it—"fat." I've heard it all my life. But no more, huh-uh. I got my act together.

CANDY: How in the world did you do it?

LORRAINE: Lots of little things, really. What really helped, though, was meeting a man I liked a lot. He was fat, too. But we encouraged each other and helped each other out, kinda like Alcoholics Anonymous. And guess what? We're getting married! That's why I came up—so I could shop for a wedding dress.

Candy is agog; she can't believe it.

CANDY: Well, I'll be a… Congratulations, Lorraine. I'm really glad for you. Excuse my manners, this is my friend Rhonda Jeffries. We were just talking about obesity on the way home.

Rhonda says hi.

CANDY: We bought this little booklet. I was gonna give it to you, but I think I'll keep it for myself now...

Fade out as they gather Candy's groceries and head for the house.

Answers and Explanations

1st Intermission

1. Darrell is not interested in hearing Mr. John's boxing stories.
2. Darrell says that he's heard Mr. John's boxing stories "10 or 12 times, maybe even more." He also says, "Not now!" From this you can guess that Darrell is not interested in hearing them again.
3. Mr. John infers that someone's apartment was burglarized.
4. Mr. John makes this inference by noticing the following details:
   (a) someone being carried out on a stretcher from a project building
   (b) a ransacked apartment
   (c) a broken door
5. Darrell brings Mr. John the article because there have been a lot of burglaries in Mr. John's neighborhood.
6. Mr. John is not interested in what Darrell has to say.
7. Mr. John says, "You woke me up for that?" Mr. John then falls asleep. From this you can infer that Mr. John is not interested in what Darrell has to say.
8. Candy asks Rhonda, "What are you going to get? A Cadillac or a Continental?" Rhonda answers, "Fat chance. No, it would have to be a clunker. Something for a couple hundred dollars." From this you can infer that Cadillacs and Continentals are expensive.
9. The car ad states that the body is "fair but needs work." From this you can infer that the body is probably damaged to some extent.
10. Candy at first does not approve of Rhonda's eagerness to buy the car.
11. Candy says, "I don't know, Rhonda. That guaranteed satisfaction could turn out to be a guaranteed hassle." From this you can infer that Candy does not think Rhonda should rush out and buy the car.

Passage 1

1. The first sentence states that burglar alarms fall into two categories: perimeter systems and ultrasonic systems.

2. (b) You can infer that the sensors used under rugs are different from the sensors used in windows.
3. The third sentence of the perimeter system section states that special sensors are available for under carpets, rugs, and stairtread coverings. Thus, you can infer that these special sensors are not the same as the sensors used in windows.
4. (d) You can infer that sensors are not used in the ultrasonic system.
5. The passage states that in the ultrasonic system, a transmitter sends out a signal that covers a cone-shaped area. Sensors are not mentioned. Thus, you can infer that sensors are not used in the ultrasonic system.
6. You can infer that the perimeter system requires the most installation work. In the perimeter system, sensors must be installed in various places. No installation work is mentioned for the ultrasonic system.

Passage 2

1. The passage states that if you don't lose your unwanted weight, you could get $1,000.
2. The passage states that the "Weight Loss Success Certificate" is backed by "the World Famous London Insurer."
3. (a) You can infer that the company accepts credit cards.
4. The pictures of the two credit cards lead you to infer that the company accepts credit cards.
5. (b) You can infer that not everyone who doesn't lose their unwanted weight will receive $1,000.
6. The passage states that if you don't lose your unwanted weight, you could get $1,000. Also, the passage states that the $1,000 offer is "in accordance with the terms of Weight Loss Success Certificate." From this information you can infer that not everyone who doesn't lose their unwanted weight will receive $1,000.

Passage 3

1. (c) You can infer that vinegar is sometimes used to clean automatic drip coffeemakers.
2. The next-to-last sentence compares the price of Drip Clean, which is an automatic drip coffeemaker cleaner, to the price of vinegar. From this you can infer that vinegar also is used to clean automatic drip coffeemakers.

3. (a) You can infer that water contains minerals.
4. The first sentence of the passage states that water leaves mineral deposits in automatic drip coffeemakers. In order for water to leave mineral deposits, it must contain minerals.

2nd Intermission

Passage 4

1. The third sentence of the passage states that the landlord may have to show your dwelling to prospective purchasers, lenders, tenants, workmen, or contractors.
2. (b) The topic of the passage is right of entry or access. The passage as a whole explains the situations in which the landlord may enter or have access to your dwelling.
3. (d) The next-to-last sentence states that the landlord should come at reasonable hours and at your convenience except in an emergency. From this you can infer that the landlord can enter your dwelling at any time if there is an emergency.
4. (c) The last sentence states that the exact wording of the right of entry should be checked before you sign your lease. This implies that if you are not satisfied with the right-of-entry section of your lease, you should not sign the lease. From this you can infer that the right of entry takes effect once you sign the lease.

Passage 5

1. The passage states that creditors look for these signs of stability: how long you've lived at your present address, whether you own or rent, and whether you are insured.
2. The last sentence of the passage states that savings, investments, or property can be used to repay the loan.
3. The passage as a whole explains that creditors look for ability to repay the loan, stable character, and other sources aside from income to repay the loan. The sentence that best states this is the first sentence: *Creditors look for an ability to repay debt and a willingness to do so—and sometimes for a little extra security to protect their loans.*
4. (d) Under "Capacity," the passage states that creditors want to know your occupation, how long you've worked, and how

much money you make. This implies that creditors will consider you for a loan only if you have a job and you earn a salary. Thus, you can infer that the creditor probably will not give you a loan if you are unemployed.

5. (a) Under "Character," the passage states that the creditor looks for signs of stability. It states that the creditor will want to know how long you have lived at your present address. This implies that one sign of stability is if you've lived at your present address for a while. From this you can infer that a person who moves frequently does not show signs of stability and may have a hard time getting a loan.
6. (b) Under "Collateral," the passage states that creditors look for sources other than income for repaying your loan. From this you can infer that if you do have these other sources, it will be easier for you to get a loan.

Passage 6

1. The first sentence states that household products and medicines should be stored in a locked cabinet or closet.
2. The seventh section of the passage states that to clean out old medicine, you should
   (1) flush the medicine down the drain;
   (2) rinse the container in water; and
   (3) discard the container.
3. (a) In several places the passage emphasizes the importance of keeping medicines and household products away from children. From this you can conclude that children should not have access to household products and medicine.
4. (c) The sixth section of the passage explains that you should not imply that medicine is candy. Since children like candy, you can infer that some children eat and drink medicine because they think it is candy.

After the Show

Vocabulary Review

1. *Stabilizers* are additives that are used to improve and maintain the quality of foods.

2. *Infer* means to come to a conclusion based on evidence.
3. *Burglary* is the act of breaking into a home for the purpose of stealing valuables.
4. A *humidifier* is a machine that adds moisture to the air.
5. A *guarantee* is an insurance of the quality of a product.
6. A *symbol* is something that stands for or suggests something else.
7. *Additives* are ingredients that are added to improve the quality of foods.
8. *Ransacked* means "removed the valuables from."
9. To *repel* is to drive away.
10. *Artificial* means "not natural."
11. An *illusion* is something that fools someone into believing what is not true.
12. *Neutralizing* means "taking away the effect of."
13. An *infection* is the condition that results when the body is invaded by a disease-producing substance.
14. To *defy* is to refuse to cooperate with or obey.
15. *Humidity* is the amount of moisture in the air.
16. *Obsolete* means "no longer in use."
17. A *strike plate* is a metal fastening on a door frame into which the bolt of a lock fits.

Reading Skills Review

Passage 7

1. The first section of the passage states that ambulances, police cars, and fire vehicles all have red lights.
2. The first section of the passage states that when a vehicle with a red light approaches, you must get to the right-hand side of the road and stop.
3. (b) In the blue light section, the passage states that vehicles with a blue light *should* be granted the right of way. Compare this to the first section, where the passage states that when a vehicle with a red light approaches, the law says that you *must* get to the right and stop. From this you can infer that you are not required by law to get to the right and stop for a vehicle with a blue light.

Passage 8

1. The second paragraph states that Legal Aid is supplied with federal government funds; state, local, or private funds; or local bar association funds.
2. The topic of the passage is Legal Aid and Legal Services. The passage as a whole explains that *Legal Aid and Legal Services provide legal services for people who can't afford private lawyers.*
3. The sentence that best states the main idea is the first sentence: *Legal Aid and Legal Services offices help people who cannot afford to hire private lawyers and who meet financial eligibility requirements.*
4. (c) The last paragraph of the passage lists the types of cases that Legal Aid and Legal Services handle. Notice that they do not handle criminal cases. Thus, you can conclude that they would not handle a case in which a man is arrested and charged with assault.
5. (d) The first sentence explains that Legal Aid and Legal Services are for people who meet financial eligibility requirements. From this you can infer that before Legal Aid or Legal Services will take your case, they probably will want to know how much money you make.
6. (a) The second sentence of the second paragraph talks about funding for Legal Aid *offices*. Compare this with the third sentence of that paragraph, which talks about funding for the Legal Services *Corporation*. From this you can infer that Legal Aid is made up of individual offices and probably has no central corporation.

Passage 9

1. The passage states that if you don't think you can afford something, don't buy it.
2. The passage mentions gasoline and other energy products as examples of products that are in short supply.
3. Answers may vary, but your answer should read something like: *You can save money and help fight inflation if you follow several shopping tips*. The passage as a whole gives these shopping tips.
4. (a) The last sentence of the passage states that you should try to save some of your income if you possibly can. From this you can infer that saving some of your income is not easy.

5. (c) The first sentence of the last section of the passage states that you should live within your means. The passage goes on to imply that this means that you should not take on more personal debt (in other words, what you spend) than you can handle. From this you can infer that "living within your means" means not spending more than you earn.

Passage 10

1. The passage states that if someone offers you something for nothing, you can bet you're going to get nothing for something.
2. The passage states that if you are pressured to sign a contract, you should wait, read it over, take it to a lawyer, or ask the Better Business Bureau for advice.
3. (c) The last sentence of the passage states that in most states you can change your mind within three days after you sign the contract. From this you can conclude that you can't call off the contract anytime after three days.
4. (a) The passage states that if you learn to recognize fraud, you won't fall for it. This implies that if you don't recognize fraud or con artists' tricks, you may fall for them. From this you can infer that the people who are not familiar with con artists' tricks are the most likely victims of fraud.
5. (c) The fourth sentence explains that con artists can be young or old or men or women. From this you can infer that you can't tell a con artist by the way he looks.
6. (c) The next-to-last section of the passage explains that you should be careful when asked to sign a contract. Since the passage as a whole is about fraud, you can infer that contracts can be written in such a way that you will fall victim to fraud, or lose money.

Passage 11

1. The writer probably does not agree with the theories of evolution.
2. The description of the book being offered explains that the book gives overwhelming evidence in favor of creation. Also, notice that the word DENY is emphasized. From this information you can infer that the writer looks down on those who deny the Biblical account of creation.
3. The writer probably does not agree that children should be taught that they descended from apes.

4. Again, the description of the book, which gives evidence in favor of creation, is a clue. Also, notice that the word APES is emphasized. From this you can infer that the writer looks down on those who believe the theory of evolution.
5. The writer probably does not agree that evolutionists should be able to prevent the teaching of the Biblical account of creation.
6. Once again, the description of the book is a clue. Also, notice that the writer refers to the *evolutionists*. By doing this, the writer implies that he is not an evolutionist. He also emphasizes the word *PREVENT*. From this information you can infer that the writer looks down on the evolutionists who prevent the teaching of the Biblical account of creation.

5

Using Sources of Information

In this program, you will see how to find information about a certain topic. You will see how to find and use sources of information.

Videotape Preview

The videotape you are about to watch is divided into three parts. In the first part, Darrell sees what he thinks is a UFO and decides he wants to learn more about UFOs. Mr. John tells Darrell how to find out more about the subject. Also in the first part, Rhonda wants to visit her mother but doesn't know how to get to her mother's house.

"The Inside Story" will demonstrate how you can find useful information in books.

In the third part of the tape, Darrell's ability to find and use sources of information makes him an "expert" on UFOs. Also in the third part, Bobby helps Rhonda get to her mother's house by showing Rhonda how to read a map.

As you watch the first section of the tape, try to answer the following questions:

- Why does Darrell want to learn more about UFOs?
- Where does Mr. John say Darrell should start his investigation?
- Mr. John tells Darrell to write down some useful sources of information that can be found in the library. What are these sources of information?
- What does Rhonda say has helped her learn to fix her car?
- What does Rhonda say she will get before she goes to visit her mother?

Vocabulary

The following words are used on the tape and in this lesson. Before you watch the tape or do any work in this lesson, study the meanings of these words:

category: a general group or class in which something belongs
Chicken and turkey are grouped under the ***category*** *"poultry."*

coordinates: a number and letter used to locate a point on a map
The map's index lists the ***coordinates*** *of Dodge City as A5.*

definition: the meaning of a word or expression
If you are unsure of the meaning of a word, you can look up its ***definition*** *in the dictionary.*

enamel: a paint that, when dry, has a glossy, or shiny, appearance
Enamel *is used to paint surfaces that should look shiny.*

exterior: outside
In order to paint the outside of your home, you must use ***exterior*** *paint.*

interior: inside
In order to paint the walls inside your home, you must use ***interior*** *paint.*

investigation: a search for information

When the police need to find the facts about a case, they conduct an ***investigation****.*

legend: the section of a map that explains the symbols used on the map

According to the map's ***legend****, a circle with a star inside it represents a capital city.*

librarian: a person who works in a library

The ***librarian*** *told me that the* Reader's Guide to Periodicals *will help me find magazine articles about UFOs.*

manual: a small guide or instruction book

You can find instructions for using a camera in the owner's ***manual****.*

periodical: magazines and journals that are issued on a regular basis

Magazines are called ***periodicals*** *because they come out periodically, or regularly.*

phenomenon: a fact or event that can be seen

An erupting geyser is a ***phenomenon*** *of nature.*

private eye: a person who investigates crimes

The ***private eye*** *asked each of the witnesses to give a description of the bank robber.*

reference book: a book that contains useful information

A dictionary, which lists the definitions of words, is an example of a ***reference book****.*

scale: a divided line on a map or chart that indicates units of measurement

According to the ***scale****, one inch on the map equals one mile.*

source: a book or person that supplies information

An encyclopedia is a ***source*** *of detailed information about various topics.*

stimulant: a substance that increases the rate of activity
*Because the caffeine in coffee is a **stimulant**, many people drink coffee in the morning to wake themselves up.*

term: a word or words used in a specific field
*Scientific **terms** tend to be long and hard to pronounce.*

UFO: an unidentified flying object
*Many **UFO** sightings have not been fully explained.*

Watch Part 1

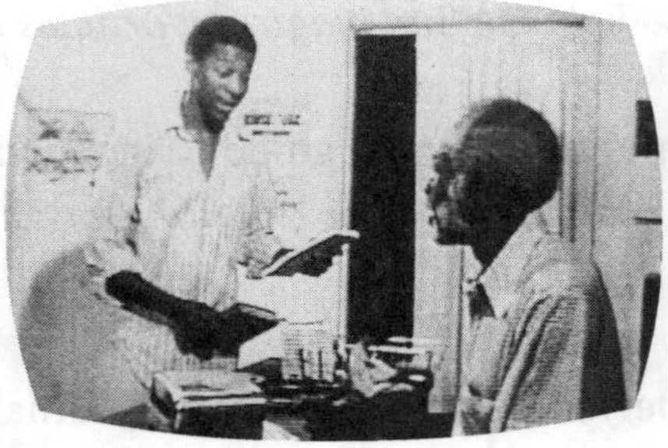

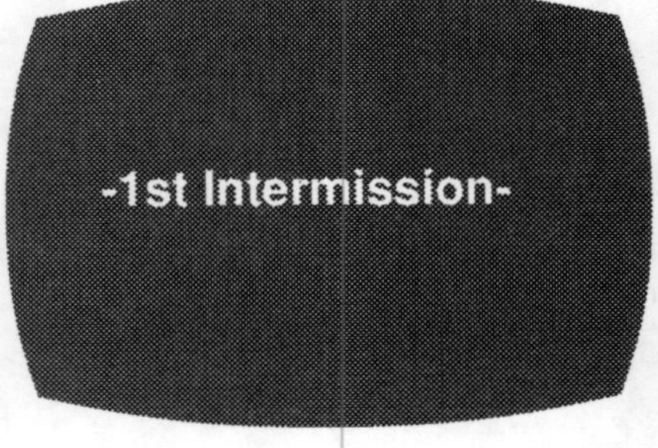

Suppose your car needs to go to a mechanic for repairs. How can you make sure you won't be overcharged?

Or suppose you have to buy a prescription drug for a member of your family. You go to the drugstore and are surprised to find out how expensive the medicine is. Is there any way to get the same prescription drug at a lower price?

How do you find the answers to these questions? Where can you look for useful information that will make you a smarter consumer?

Well, you could go to the library, start with the first book you see, and read the entire book cover to cover. If that book didn't provide the information you were looking for, you could go on to the next book. And you could repeat the process until you found what you were looking for.

But think about how many books there are in a library. It could take years to find the information you needed. Then again, you might never find what you were looking for.

There is an easier way. You can learn to use the materials that will help you narrow down the thousands of books in the library to the few books you will need. And you can learn how to narrow down an entire book to the few chapters or pages that deal specifically with the information you are looking for.

The following exercise is based on the situations on the tape.

1. Why does Darrell want to learn more about UFOs?

2. Where does Mr. John say Darrell should start his investigation?

3. Who does Mr. John suggest Darrell go to for help in the library?

4. Mr. John tells Darrell to write down some useful sources of information that can be found in the library. What are these sources of information?

5. What does Rhonda say has helped her learn how to fix her car?

6. What's wrong with the directions that Rhonda's mother gives Rhonda?

7. What do you think would happen if Rhonda tried to get to her mother's without using a map?

8. What does Rhonda say she will get before she goes to visit her mother?

Check your answers on page 100

The most important thing you need to know in order to find and use sources of information is how alphabetical order works. The library card catalogue, dictionaries, encyclopedias, indexes, glossaries, and bibliographies are all arranged in alphabetical order.

When something is in alphabetical order, it is arranged according to the letters of the alphabet:

A B C D E F G H I J K L M N O P Q R S T U V W X Y Z

When something is in alphabetical order, words that begin with the letter A are listed before words that begin with the letter B, since

A comes before B in the alphabet. Words that begin with the letter G are listed before words that begin with the letter M, since G comes before M in the alphabet.

Arrange the following words in alphabetical order:

Beverages	Cakes
Salads	Vegetables
Appetizers	Fish

The correct alphabetical arrangement is Appetizers, Beverages, Cakes, Fish, Salads, Vegetables. A comes before B, B comes before C, C comes before F, F comes before S, and S comes before V.

If more than one word in a list begins with the same letter, look at the second letter of each word. The second letter determines the order of the words when the words begin with the same letter. For example, "cakes" would come before "cereals" because A comes before E in the alphabet. "Salads" would come before "soups" because A comes before O in the alphabet.

Remember, you look at the second letters only if the first letters are the same. And if both the first and the second letters are the same, you must look at the third letter, and so on. For example, "salads" would come before "sauces" because L comes before U in the alphabet. "Soufflés" would come before "soups" because the first three letters of these words are the same and the fourth letter of "soufflés" (F) comes before the fourth letter of "soups" (P).

Exercise 1

Cookies	Cereals
Shellfish	Cakes
Vegetables	Poultry
Sauces	Fruits
Meat	Salads

1. Arrange the above words in alphabetical order.

Check your answers on page 101

Exercise 2

The following list is taken from a newspaper index:

Art	12A
Books	17A
Business	19-21
Editorials	1A
Living	19A
Music	21A-22A
Obituaries	22
People	20A
Real Estate	24A-25A
Society	27A
Theater	7A-9A
TV	15A
Weather	28A

1. Between what two words should *Crossword* go?

2. Between what two words should *Movies* go?

3. Between what two words should *Sports* go?

Check your answers on page 101

When you are using a reference book that is arranged in alphabetical order, *guide words* help you locate information faster. Guide words tell you the first and last words on the page. You know that any word that alphabetically comes between the guide words is on that page. The dictionary is a reference book that uses guide words:

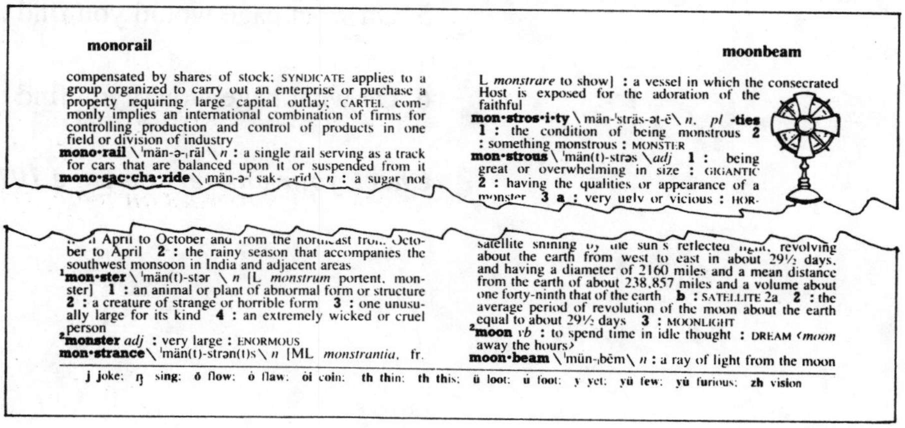

monorail **moonbeam**

compensated by shares of stock; SYNDICATE applies to a group organized to carry out an enterprise or purchase a property requiring large capital outlay; CARTEL commonly implies an international combination of firms for controlling production and control of products in one field or division of industry
mono·rail \ˈmän-ə-ˌrāl\ *n* : a single rail serving as a track for cars that are balanced upon it or suspended from it
mono·sac·cha·ride \ˌmän-ə-ˈsak-ə-ˌrīd\ *n* : a sugar not

... April to October and from the northeast from October to April **2** : the rainy season that accompanies the southwest monsoon in India and adjacent areas
[1]**mon·ster** \ˈmän(t)-stər\ *n* [L *monstrum* portent, monster] **1** : an animal or plant of abnormal form or structure **2** : a creature of strange or horrible form **3** : one unusually large for its kind **4** : an extremely wicked or cruel person
[2]**monster** *adj* : very large : ENORMOUS
mon·strance \ˈmän(t)-strən(t)s\ *n* [ML *monstrantia*, fr. L *monstrare* to show] : a vessel in which the consecrated Host is exposed for the adoration of the faithful
mon·stros·i·ty \män-ˈsträs-ət-ē\ *n*, *pl* **-ties** **1** : the condition of being monstrous **2** : something monstrous : MONSTER
mon·strous \ˈmän(t)-strəs\ *adj* **1** : being great or overwhelming in size : GIGANTIC **2** : having the qualities or appearance of a monster **3 a** : very ugly or vicious : HOR-

satellite shining by the sun's reflected light, revolving about the earth from west to east in about 29½ days, and having a diameter of 2160 miles and a mean distance from the earth of about 238,857 miles and a volume about one forty-ninth that of the earth **b** : SATELLITE 2a **2** : the average period of revolution of the moon about the earth equal to about 29½ days **3** : MOONLIGHT
[2]**moon** *vb* : to spend time in idle thought : DREAM ‹*moon* away the hours›
moon·beam \ˈmün-ˌbēm\ *n* : a ray of light from the moon

j joke; **ŋ** sing; **ō** flow; **ȯ** flaw; **ȯi** coin; **th** thin; **th** this; **ü** loot; **u̇** foot; **y** yet; **yü** few; **yu̇** furious; **zh** vision

In this example, the guide words are located at the top of the page and are in dark type. The guide words are *monorail* and *moonbeam.* This tells you that *monorail* is the first word on the page and that *moonbeam* is the last word on the page. Since the words in a dictionary are in alphabetical order, you know that any word that falls between *monorail* and *moonbeam* will be found on this page. For example, the words *monotony*, *monsoon*, and *montage* would all be found on this page. The words *monolith* and *mosaic* do not fall between *monorail* and *moonbeam.* Thus, they would be found on other pages of the dictionary.

Exercise 3

The following guide words are taken from a dictionary:

federalist	**fellow**	p. 309
fellow	**ferret**	p. 310
ferret	**fetter**	p. 311
fettle	**fiddled**	p. 312

1. On what page would you find the definition of the word *fiction*?

2. On what page would you find the definition of the word *fiat*?

3. On what page would you find the definition of the word *femur*?

4. On what page would you find the definition of the word *federalize*?

5. On what page would you find the definition of the word *festoon*?

6. On what page would you find the definition of the word *ferment*?

Check your answers on page 101

Guide words also are used in the white pages of a telephone directory. The white pages are arranged alphabetically by the names of people and businesses in the area. Here's an excerpt from the white pages:

BONOMI-BOREK

Bonomi Mary Mrs 1120 26	854-6161
Bonomo Angelina 63 Franklin	389-2432
Bonomo Anthony J 127 West	853-8716
Bonomo Bennie 49 E23	531-3052
Bonomo Frank 321 88	788-6001
Bonomo Giuseppe 129 Gordon	996-5312
Bonomo I 41 Elm	891-4100
Bonomo Patk J 165 Main	259-6281
Bonomo Salvatore 185 31	436-6835
Bonomo Vincent 17 63	256-9212
Bonomo Wm J 77 Sunset	389-0079
Bonomolo Ernest furn refnshg 17 Taft	891-1826
Bonomolo Frank 109 31	833-1292
Bonomolo Grace Mrs 1732 Main	331-3131

Exercise 4

Look at the following guide words from a telephone directory:

LATTING	LAURO	p. 536
LAURO	LAWRENCE	p. 537
LAWRENCE	LAZARUS	p. 538
LAZARUS	LEBOVIC	p. 539

1. On what page would you find the telephone number for a person whose last name is Lawson?

2. On what page would you find the telephone number for a person whose last name is Leahy?

3. On what page would you find the telephone number for a person whose last name is Lau?

4. On what page would you find the telephone number for a person whose last name is Lasky?

5. On what page would you find the telephone number for a person whose last name is Lawn?

6. On what page would you find the telephone number for a person whose last name is Laurence?

Check your answers on page 101

Another important skill that will help you find and use sources of information is finding a general category from a specific item. Suppose you want to buy a night-light. The first thing to do is to find out who sells night-lights. You look under N in the yellow pages of your telephone directory and find no listing for night-lights. This is because a night-light is too specific an item to have its own heading in the yellow pages. You must look under a more general *category*. Stores that sell night-lights and other lights are listed under the general category *lighting fixtures*. Rather than list individual items, the yellow pages section lists general categories in alphabetical order.

Here's an excerpt from the yellow pages:

Restaurants (Cont'd)

SANTINO'S RESTAURANT & COCKTAIL LOUNGE 17 Main **593-9786**

Santino's Restaurant & Cocktail Lounge
36 Archer 599-6710

Santosha Vegetarian Dining Plus
17 Amity 598-2694

SAPPORO JAPANESE RESTAURANT
Authentic Japanese Cuisine
See our display ad Page 1078
1877 Hyde **746-3031**

Sasaki Japanese Restaurant
405 Carle 334-8444

SAVINI'S CRYSTALBROOK
Catering Organizational Luncheons
Dinners, Affairs, Elegant Catering
201 Meadow **794-9516**

Savino's Italian Cuisine
114 Sunset 593-1787

SAXON ARMS RESTAURANT
Waterfront Patio Dining, Continental-American
31 Oakdale **589-9306**

Exercise 5

Match the specific items on the left with the general categories on the right.

___ 1. grape juice	A. Apparel—Women's
___ 2. skirt	B. Bathroom Accessories
___ 3. carburetor	C. Pet Supplies and Foods
___ 4. animal cage	D. Signs
___ 5. neon sign	E. Automobile Parts and Supplies
___ 6. soap dish	F. Beverages

Check your answers on page 102

Finding a general category for a specific item is not always easy. It often involves a lot of guesswork. Sometimes, a reference book will help you find a general category from a specific item. Here are some examples from the yellow pages:

Dog Pounds—See "Animal Shelters"
Epoxy Adhesives—See "Adhesives and Glues"
Gasoline Meters—See "Meters"
Stereo and High Fidelity Equipment—See also "Automobile Radios and Stereo Systems"

These instructions are called *cross-references*. They tell you to look in another area of the book for the information you need.

Read the following passage. Then answer the questions that follow the passage.

Exercise 6

The following is a directory of a department store:

	Floor
Appliances—Small	5
Appliances—Major	4
Artists' Supplies	6
Books	6
Cooking Equipment	3
Furniture	7
Lingerie	2
Menswear	1
Shoes—Men's	1
Shoes—Women's	2
Sporting Goods	6
Swimwear—Men's	1
Swimwear—Women's	2
Toys	6
Women's Apparel	2

1. Between what two words should *Hats* go?

2. Between what two words should *Jewelry* go?

3. Between what two words should *Hardware* go?

4. On what floor would you find an egg-beater?

5. On what floor would you find a necktie?

6. On what floor would you find a hair dryer?

7. On what floor would you find a sofa?

8. On what floor would you find a dictionary?

Check your answers on page 102

Watch Part 2:
"The Inside Story"

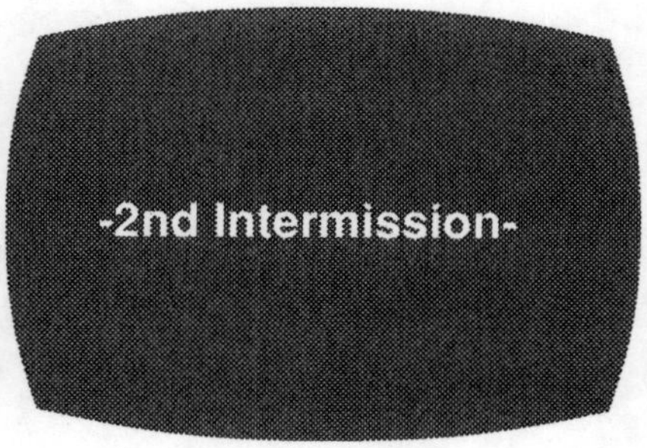

The Library

Suppose you go to the library to look for information about the price of prescription drugs. How do you know where in the library you will find your source of information? If you're looking for a book, the first thing to do is to look in the card catalogue.

The card catalogue is made up of drawers of small cards. There are three types of cards in the card catalogue: subject cards, title cards, and author cards. All of the cards are arranged in alphabetical order. If you are interested in a certain subject, you can look up the subject in the card catalogue. If you know the title of the book you are interested in, you can look up the title in the card catalogue. If you are interested in a certain author, you can look up the author's last name in the card catalogue.

Each book in the library is given at least three cards in the card catalogue—one for each type of card. Here's an example:

Subject Card

CONSUMER EDUCATION

RC 81 .M490 1980 — The Medicine Show: Consumers Union's practical guide to some everyday health problems and health products/by the editors of Consumer Reports Books. 5th ed.—New York: Pantheon Books, 1980.

383 p. includes index

1. Medicine, Popular 2. Quacks and Quackery
3. Health Products 4. Consumer Education
I. Author—Consumer Reports II. Title

Title Card

	Medicine Show, The
RC 81 .M490 1980	The Medicine Show: Consumers Union's practical guide to some everyday health problems and health products/by the editors of Consumer Reports Books. 5th ed.—New York: Pantheon Books, 1980.
	383 p. Includes index
	1. Medicine, Popular 2. Quacks and Quackery 3. Health Products 4. Consumer Education I. Author—Consumer Reports

Author Card

	Consumer Reports
RC 81 .M490 1980	The Medicine Show: Consumers Union's practical guide to some everyday health problems and health products/by the editors of Consumer Reports Books. 5th ed.—New York: Pantheon Books, 1980.
	383 p. Includes index
	1. Medicine, Popular 2. Quacks and Quackery 3. Health Products 4. Consumer Education II. Title

Subject Card: The first line of a subject card is the subject, or topic, of the book. The card is filed in the card catalogue according to the subject of the book. Thus, this subject card would be found under C for *Consumer Education*.

Title Card: The first line of a title card is the title of the book. The card is filed in the card catalogue according to the title of the book. (If the title begins with the word *The* or the word *A*, the next word is used to file the card in the card catalogue.) Thus, this title card would be found under M for *Medicine Show*.

Author Card: The first line of an author card is the author's name. (In this example, the author is considered to be Consumer Reports. This is because the book was written by a number of people from Consumer Reports Books.) Author cards are filed in the card catalogue according to the author's last name. Thus, this author card would be found under C for *Consumer Reports*.

Aside from these differences, all three cards provide the same information:

- **the book's call number:** This is the number at the left. Each book in the library has its own call number. In this example, the call number is *RC 81 .M490 1980.*
- **the full title of the book:** In this example, the full title of the book is *The Medicine Show: Consumers Union's practical guide to some everyday health problems and health products.*
- **the author of the book:** In this example, the author is *Consumer Reports.*
- **the edition of the book:** In this example, this is the *fifth edition* of the book.
- **where, when, and by whom the book was published:** In this example, the book was published in *New York* in *1980* by *Pantheon Books.*
- **the number of pages in the book:** In this example, the book has *383 pages.*
- **other useful information about the book:** In this example, the card tells you that the book has an index.
- **where else in the card catalogue the book is listed:** In this example, the book has a total of four subject cards, one author card, and one title card.

Once you find the book you want, jot down the call number, the title, and the author's name. In some libraries, the librarian gets the book for you. Before the librarian will get the book, you must fill out a form like the one below.

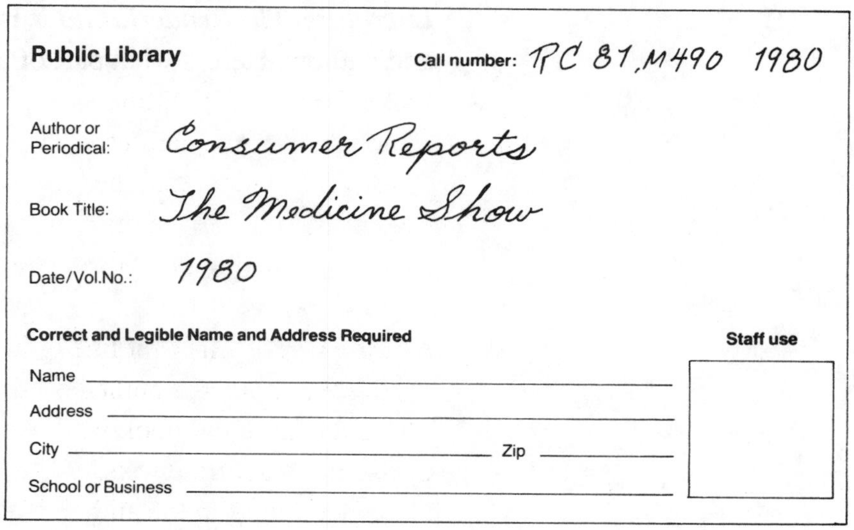
Public Library Call number: RC 81.M490 1980

Author or Periodical: Consumer Reports

Book Title: The Medicine Show

Date/Vol.No.: 1980

Correct and Legible Name and Address Required **Staff use**

Name

Address

City Zip

School or Business

In other libraries, you must find the book yourself. These libraries are called open-stack libraries. An open-stack library has a directory that will help you find the book you need. Here's a sample directory:

Call Numbers	**Floor**
A, B, C, D	4
E, F, G	5
H	8
J, K, L	10
M	2
N, P-PM	7
PN-PZ	6
Q, R, S, T, U, V	9
Z	Mezz.
Periodicals	1
Reference	3

Since the call number of the book you want begins with the letter R, you will find the book on the 9th floor. Once you get to that floor, signs will direct you to the call number you need, and the book itself has the call number printed on it.

Now let's say you would like even more information about prescription drugs. Libraries also carry copies of magazines and journals. These are found in the *periodicals* section of the library.

In order to find a magazine article about prescription drugs, you must look in a book called *The Reader's Guide to Periodical Literature*. *The Reader's Guide* is an alphabetical list of subjects and authors. Here's what part of a page from the *Reader's Guide* looks like:

DRUG laws and regulations
See also
Drugs—Prices
DRUG metabolism. See Drugs—Metabolism
DRUG receptors
Body telling the mind [endorphin researcher C. Pert] T. Alexander. il por Fortune 102:97 S 8 '80
Tritiated imipramine binding sites are decreased in platelets of untreated depressed patients. M. S. Briley and others. bibl f il Science 209:303–5 Jl 11 '80
DRUGS
See also
Medication errors
Expert warns that visits to the drugstore can be dangerous to your health [interview by B. Rowes] J. Graedon. il pors People 14:83 – 4 + S 29 '80
Dosage
On medication. W. R. Felix. por Consumers Res Mag 63:41 Jl '80
Dosage forms
Zip-coded drugs: they are now site specific in the body [delivery systems] S. Loebl. Sci Digest 87:15–17 Je '80
Metabolism
c-Glucuronidation of the acetylenic moiety of ethchlorvynol in the rabbit. C. R. Abolin and others. bibl f il Science 209:703–4 Ag 8 '80
Physiological effects
See also
Drugs-Metabolism
Some do's and don'ts of food and pills [views of Joseph Cornell] USA Today 109:2–3 Ag '80
Watch out! These medicines can hurt your eyes. J. B. Hooper. Good H 191:213 Ag '80
When drugs act up, they take notice [FDA's division of Drug Experience] W. Grigg. il FDA Consumer 14:20–3 Jl/Ag '80
Prices
Generic drugs: Rx for ripoff? M. Sheils. Newsweek 96:71–2 S 29 '80

Since you're interested in the prices of prescription drugs, you would look under the heading DRUGS and under the subheading *Prices*. There you find the following entry:

> Generic drugs: Rx for ripoff? M. Sheils. Newsweek 96:71-2 S 29 '80

The name of the article is "Generic drugs: Rx for ripoff?" M. Sheils wrote the article. It appeared in the magazine *Newsweek*, volume 96, pages 71-72. And the date of the issue in which the article appeared was September 29, 1980.

In order to get a copy of the magazine, you may have to fill out a Periodical Request Form like the one below:

PERIODICAL REQUEST FORM

Name of Periodical: *Newsweek*

Dates wanted: *September 29, 1980*

Your name: ______________________

Once you have filled out the form, give it to the librarian. The librarian will get the magazine for you. In some libraries, you must look on the shelves for the periodical. Also, sometimes all of one year's issues for a certain periodical are bound like a book. If you are unsure of where to find these periodicals, ask the librarian for help.

Useful Reference Books

Knowing how to use the following books also will help you find many practical kinds of information. All of these books can be found in the library.

Dictionary: A dictionary lists words in alphabetical order. In a dictionary you will find:

- the correct spelling of the word you are looking for
- the correct pronunciation of the word
- the part of speech of the word (noun, verb, adjective, adverb, etc.)
- various forms of the word
- the way the word developed
- the definition or definitions of the word (sometimes you will find the word used in a phrase or sentence)

Here's a sample dictionary entry:

> **ge-ner-ic**/je-ner-ik/ *adj* [F *générique*, fr. **L** *gener-*, *genus* birth, kind, class] **1 a:** relating to or characteristic of a whole group or class: GENERAL **b:** not protected by trademark registration **2:** relating to or having the rank of a biological genus *syn* see UNIVERSAL—**ge-ner-i-cal-ly**/-i-k(e-)l¯e/*adv*—**ge-ner-ic-ness** *n*

- the correct spelling of the word is g-e-n-e-r-i-c
- the correct pronunciation of the word is *jenerik* (the pronunciation guide at the bottom of each page of the dictionary explains what the pronunciation symbols mean)
- the part of speech of the word is an *adj*, or adjective
- *generically*, an adverb, and *genericness*, a noun, are two forms of the word
- the word comes from the French word *générique* and from the Latin root *gener-* and word *genus*, which means birth, kind, or class
- the word has three slightly different definitions

Encyclopedia: An encyclopedia lists topics in alphabetical order. An encyclopedia contains short articles that give information about various topics. Here's a sample entry:

> **drugs**, substances used in medicine either externally or internally for curing, alleviating, or preventing a disease or deficiency. At the turn of the century only a few medically effective substances were widely used scientifically, among them ETHER, MORPHINE, DIGITALIS, diphtheria antitoxin, smallpox vaccine, IRON, QUININE, IODINE, alcohol, and MERCURY. Since then, and particularly since World War II, many important new drugs have been developed, making chemotherapy an important part of medical practice: the ANTIBIOTICS, acting against bacteria and fungi; QUINACRINE and other synthetics acting against malaria and other parasitic infections; cardiovascular drugs, including various digitalislike agents, used in heart disease; DIURETICS, which increase the rate of urine flow; whole blood, plasma, and blood derivatives; ANTICOAGULANTS such as HEPARIN and coumarin (DICUMAROL); various smooth muscle relaxants such as PAPAVERINE, used in heart and vascular diseases; smooth muscle stimulants; immunologic agents, which protect against many diseases and allergenic substances; hormones such as THYROXINE, INSULIN, and ESTROGEN and other sex hormones; CORTISONE and synthetic CORTICOSTEROID DRUGS used in treating inflammatory diseases such as arthritis; vitamins; poison antidotes; and various drugs

that act as STIMULANTS or DEPRESSANTS on all or various parts of the nervous system.

An entry in an encyclopedia first gives a short description of the topic. It then goes on to give detailed information about the topic. Remember, a dictionary basically gives the *definitions* and *spellings* of words, while an encyclopedia gives *detailed information* about topics.

Atlas: An atlas is a collection of maps. It can be a world atlas, which is a collection of maps of the various continents and countries of the world. An atlas also can be a collection of maps of the various states or provinces in a country. Or it can be a road atlas, which is a collection of maps of smaller areas—for example, counties or cities—that show the roads you need to take to get from one place to another.

Almanac: An almanac lists facts and statistics for just about anything you can think of—population, the economy, education, sports, elections, etc. It also contains other useful information about countries, states, various associations and societies, weights and measures, etc.

Newspaper: A newspaper contains world, national, and local news; business news; sports news; entertainment news and listings; fashion news; puzzles; and editorials (editorials are short essays that give opinions on various topics of interest). Most libraries carry a *newspaper index*. The newspaper index lists the contents of back issues of newspapers. These newspapers are kept on microfilm. In order to look at a newspaper that is on microfilm, you must use a special machine found in the library.

Map: Individual maps can show countries, bus routes, train routes, or roads. On a map, roads usually are represented by lines. (Remember, an atlas is a collection of many maps.)

Using the Books

Once you locate the book you need, the following parts of the book will help you find the specific information you need:

Table of Contents: Most books (other than books like dictionaries and encyclopedias, which are arranged in alphabetical order) are divided into chapters. Each chapter deals with a specific topic. The table of contents lists the names of the chapters of a book and gives the page numbers on which the chapters begin. The table of contents usually is found in the front of a book. The table of contents is arranged according to the order in which the chapters appear. Thus, the first chapter of the book is listed first, and the last chapter of the book is listed last. Here's a sample table of contents:

If you were interested in saving money when buying prescription drugs, you might find useful information in chapter 30—*How to buy prescription drugs*. This chapter begins on page 314.

If you were interested in losing weight, you might find useful information in chapter 22—*Weight loss: diets, drugs, and devices.* This chapter begins on page 208.

(In most cookbooks, the table of contents lists categories of recipes in the order in which they usually are eaten. Thus, drinks and appetizers come first, and desserts come last.)

Index: An index is an alphabetized list of specific topics covered in a book. The index usually is found in the back of a book. The index is more detailed than the table of contents. The table of contents lists only chapters, or major divisions, of a book. The index lists specific topics that may be mentioned only once in an entire book. Here's an excerpt from an index:

Eichert, Herbert, **205-206**
Electroconvulsive therapy, **268**
Electroshock therapy, **268**
Elgin (Ill.) State Hospital, **201**
Emotional disorders, **107, 109, 153, 211-12, 256-79**
Endocrine Society, **194**

If you were interested in how to buy prescription drugs, you would look under *Drugs, prescription, how to buy*. This topic is discussed on pages 314-322.

If you were particularly interested in how you can save money by using generic drugs and whether these drugs are as effective as other drugs, you would look under *Drugs, generic*. This topic is discussed on pages 318-321.

Notice that in an index you often must look under a general *category* to find what you need. In the above example, *generic drugs* were not listed under G for generic. There was no *heading* for generic drugs. They were listed under the general category *Drugs*. The *subheading* (which is found underneath or beside the major *heading*) *generic* narrowed down the category to particular types of drugs.

(In a cookbook, the index usually lists specific recipes in alphabetical order. However, some recipes are listed under general categories. For example, *blue cheese dressing* may be listed under salad dressings.)

Glossary: A glossary is an alphabetical list of words and terms. It usually is found in the back of a book. A glossary, like a dictionary, gives the definitions of these words and terms. However, the only words in a glossary are words that are used in the book. Also, unlike a dictionary, a glossary usually gives only the definition of the word. Here's an excerpt from a glossary:

GEL. A substance of jellylike consistency.

GENERIC. Describing the name given to a **drug** by the United States Adopted Name Council (see Chapter 30), as distinct from the registered brand name a pharmaceutical company gives to its version of the same preparation.

GERMICIDAL. Referring to chemical agents, lethal to germs, which are generally used as **topical** applications. Describes the action of certain **antiseptics**. (See also **microorganisms**.)

GLAUCOMA. A serious eye disease caused by build-up of fluid pressure in the eyeball. Simple or **chronic** glaucoma usually comes on gradually as part of the **degenerative** aging process; if untreated, it usually destroys the optic nerve, causing blindness. Closed-angle (also known as narrow-angle) or **acute** glaucoma has a sudden severe onset due to narrowing of the eyeball's natural drainage channels. Acute glaucoma is accompanied by severe pain; if untreated, it can lead to irreparable damage.

GRAIN. The apothecary's traditional unit of weight—approximately 65/1,000 of a **gram**. It is still used by doctors in prescribing—and by pharmacists in compounding—pills, powders, and potions. (See also **milligram.**)

GRAM. A unit of weight in the metric system, often used to measure **drugs** and food. Approximately 28 grams are equal to 1 ounce; 1/1,000 of a gram is a **milligram**. (See also **grain.**)

GRAM-NEGATIVE and -POSITIVE. **Bacteria** are of two varieties: Gram-positive bacteria are visible under the microscope when dyed by a certain technique—Gram's stain; Gram-negative bacteria fail to hold the color. (Named after Hans Gram, a Danish bacteriologist, not after the **gram** unit of weight.)

GRANULOMAS. Microscopic **lesions** composed of whorls of **inflammatory** tissue. Granulomas are present in such diseases as **sarcoidosis**, tuberculosis, and certain **fungal infections**.

HALLUCINOGEN. A **drug** that may in some individuals cause hallucinations, either auditory or visual.

Since this glossary is from a medical book, the glossary contains only medical words and terms. Suppose you would like to know what the word *generic* means in a medical sense. Looking at the Gs, then the G-Es, and finally at G-E-N, you will find the definition of the medical term *generic*.

Bibliography: Once you find the information you need, you may want to go to other books for more information about the same subject. Many books contain bibliographies. A bibliography usually is located at the back of a book. It is a list of other books and magazines that you can read to find out more about the topic you are interested in. The bibliography lists books in alphabetical order by author's last name (or by title if the book lists no author). Here's an excerpt from a bibliography:

Books

Historical background of consumerism can be found in:

Campbell, Persia. *Consumer representation in the New Deal.* New York, AMS Press, (1940), 1968.

Mark V. Nadel, *The politics of consumer protection.* New York, The Bobbs-Merrill Company, Inc., 1971.

Sorenson, Helen, *The consumer movement, what it is and what it means.* New York, Harper, 1941.

Frequently mentioned current books include:

Aaker, David A. *Consumerism: search for the consumer interest.* New York, The Free Press, 1971.

Buckhorn, Robert F. *Nader, the people's lawyer.* Englewood Cliffs, New Jersey, Prentice-Hall, 1972

Green, Mark J. *The closed enterprise system, Ralph Nader's study group report on antitrust enforcement.* New York, Grossman, 1972.

McCarry, Charles, *Citizen Nader.* New York, Saturday Review Press, 1972.

Taylor, Jack L. Jr. and Arch Trolstrop. *The consumer in American society: additional dimensions.* New York, 1974.

Legend: Important information about a map is listed in the map's legend. A map's legend explains what all of the symbols on the map mean. It also includes the map's scale, which indicates units of measurement on the map (for example, one inch on the map equals five miles). Here's an example of a legend:

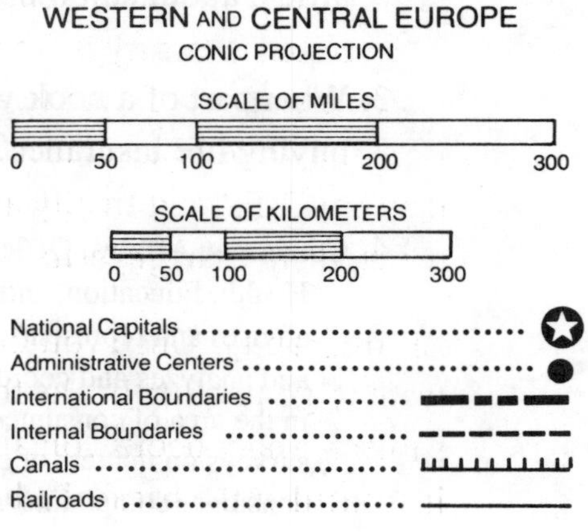

According to the legend, each inch on the map equals 100 miles. The legend also shows the symbols that are used on the map for national capitals, administrative centers, international boundaries, internal boundaries, canals, and railroads.

Scanning and Skimming

If you are using a book, such as a dictionary, that lists words in alphabetical order, you can *scan* the pages until you find what you need. When you scan, you do not read every word. Instead, you flip through the pages and check the guide words until you find the page on which the word will be found. Then, glance down the list until you come close to where the word would fall alphabetically. You then can look more closely for the word you need.

If you are not using a book that lists words in alphabetical order, use the index to find the pages on which the topic you are interested in is discussed. You can then *skim* the pages until you find what you need. When you skim, you do not read every word. Instead, you glance over the words until you find what you are looking for. Suppose you look up *generic drugs* in the index and find that they are discussed on pages 318-321. You would then turn to page 318, skim the page until you notice the word *generic*, and begin your reading there.

Exercise 7

1. In what book would you find the definition of the word *consumer*?

2. What book in the library would you use to find a magazine article about automobile repairs?

3. What part of a book would you use to find a chapter about buying life insurance?

4. **Consumer Affairs, Office of,** agency of the U.S. Department of Health, Education, and Welfare; established 1971. The office advises and represents the President on matters of consumer interest and analyzes and coordinates activities of the Federal government in the area of consumer protection. It conducts investigations and surveys on matters of consumer interest, takes action on individual consumer complaints, makes available to the public information the

government has acquired in making its own purchases, and presses for legislation to protect the consumer.

In what book would you find the above entry?

5. Where would you look to find out what the symbol —— on a map means?

6. In what book would you find a map of South America?

7. In what part of a book would you find the name of another book on the same subject?

8. What part of a book would you use to find the page numbers on which a specific topic, such as fixing flat tires, is discussed?

9. What part of a book lists the definitions of terms used in the book?

10. In what book would you look for addresses of car mechanics?

11. In what book would you find a recipe for chili?

12. [1]**mechanic** /mi-ˈkan-ik/ *adj* [Gk *mechanikos*, fr. *mechane* machine]: of or relating to manual work or skill <*mechanic* arts>
[2]**mechanic** *n*: a manual worker: ARTISAN; *esp*: a repairer of machines

In what book would you find the above entry?

13. Health care, 251-263
    birth control, 289-291
    cancer, 258-259
    costs, 251, 235-256
    dentists, 261-263
    doctors, 256-257
    drugs, 264-291
    costs of, 266-267
    mail-order, 267-269
    non-prescription, 277-289
    nursing homes, 259-261
    patients' rights, 257
    prescription, 265-274
    quality of, 251-153
    records, 253-257
    symbols, 291
    surgery, 253-256

unproven, 273-274
voting on, 50-55
Health foods, 204-205, 581
Hearing aids, 35, 282-285
Heating, home, 519, 522

In what part of a book would you find the above entry?

14.

Fowikes Ernest L 327 23	997-4718
Fowikes William 18 Ivy	546-5483
Fowls Stephen 2401 Birch	536-5409
Fowsky Frank J 116 Wilson	349-1372
Fox A 81 Garden	431-5659
Fox A 26 Park	239-5254
Fox A R C 15 Baltic	781-9202
Fox Abe 2045 71	764-4308
Fox Abraham L 83 Firehouse	486-8555
Fox Abraham L 83 Firehouse	486-2166
Fox Al N 12 Oak	569-8162
Fox Alfred F 168 Adams	223-6068
Fox Allan 55 Church	433-7834

In what book would you find the above entry?

15. Deutsch, R.M.: *The Family Guide to Better Food and Better Health.* Meredith Corporation, Des Moines, Iowa, 1971.
Fleck, H., and Munves, E.D.: *Everybody's Book of Modern Diet and Nutrition,* 2nd ed. Dell Publishing Company, New York, 1959.
Goodhart, R.S.: *Nutrition for You.* E.P. Dutton Company, New York, 1958.
Leverton, R.M.: *Food Becomes You*, 3rd ed. Iowa State University Press, Ames, 1965.
McHenry, E.W.: *Foods Without Fads.* J.B. Lippincott Company, Philadelphia, 1960.
Martin, E.A.: *Nutrition in Action,* 3rd ed. Holt, Rinehart & Winston, New York, 1971.
Robinson, C.H.: *Basic Nutrition and Diet Therapy*, 2nd ed. The Macmillan Company, New York, 1970.
Stare, F.J.: *Eating for Good Health*, Doubleday, New York, 1964.
U.S. Department of Agriculture:
Consumers All. Yearbook of Agriculture, 1965.
Food for Us All. Yearbook of Agriculture, 1969.
Food, the Yearbook of Agriculture, 1959.

In what part of a book would you find the above entry?

Check your answers on page 103

Exercise 8

1. Under which of the following subject headings would you find the card for a book that explains how to fix leaky faucets?
   (a) CARPENTRY
   (b) BANKING AND FINANCE
   (c) HOME REPAIRS
   (d) MONEY

2. Which of the following does not provide enough information to find a book in the card catalogue?
   (a) the title of the book
   (b) the author of the book
   (c) the publisher of the book
   (d) the subject of the book

3. Under what letter would the following card be filed in the card catalogue?

	Great American Auto Repair Robbery, The
TL	Randall, Donald A.
152 .R135	The Great American Auto Repair Robbery; a report on a ten billion dollar national swindle and what you can do about it by Donald A. Randall and Arthur P. Glickman. New York, Charterhouse, 1972. 235 p. illus. Includes bibliography 1. Automobiles—maintenance and repair 2. Automobile industry and trade—United States I. Author—Randall, Donald A. II. Author—Glickman, Arthur P.

   (a) R
   (b) T
   (c) A
   (d) G

4. Why is it important to know the call number of a book?

Check your answers on page 103

Exercise 9

1. What part of a book is this?

2. Beginning on what page would you be likely to find information about flat-rate manuals?

3. Beginning on what page would you be likely to find a discussion of government regulations of auto repair shops?

4. Beginning on what page would you be likely to find information about the high price of auto parts?

Check your answers on page 104

Exercise 10

1. What part of a book is this?

2. On what page would you find information about carpools?

3. On what pages would you find information about auto repairs?

4. On what pages would you find information about television commercials meant for children?

5. On what pages would you find information about getting a loan from a bank?

Check your answers on page 104

Watch Part 3

In this program you have seen:

- that you can use many different sources of information to find information about a topic
- how to use the library
- what kinds of books in the library will help you find sources of information
- what parts of the books will help you locate specific information
- that scanning and skimming can help you find the information you need

Vocabulary Review

The following vocabulary exercise is based on the vocabulary words at the beginning of this unit. For each sentence, choose the correct word from the list below and write that word in the space provided. (Each word is used only once.)

category	investigation	private eye
coordinates	legend	reference
definition	librarian	scale
enamel	manual	source
exterior	periodical	stimulant
interior	phenomenon	terms
		UFO

1. __________ is a good type of paint to use on countertops that need to look shiny.

2. A tidal wave is a natural __________.

3. The __________ that are used in this history book are the same ones that I find in the newspaper every day.

4. If you look up in the sky and think you see a __________ flying around, you should report it to the police.

5. If you are not satisfied with a police investigation into a burglary, you can go to a __________.

6. The detective didn't want anyone to know that he was conducting an __________ into the crime.

7. Crab, lobster, and shrimp all fall under the __________ of shellfish.

8. __________ paint is used to paint the outside of houses.

9. You can find magazines and journals in the __________ section of the library.

10. A __________, such as caffeine, may wake you up in the morning, but it also can make you nervous and jumpy.

11. If you are unsure of what a symbol on a map means, you should check the map's __________.

12. If you can't find what you want in the library, you can always ask the __________ for help.

13. The dictionary lists five __________ for the word credit.

14. To find a particular city on a map, check the map's index for the city's __________.

15. __________ paint is used to paint ceilings and walls inside your home.

16. Diane helped Bill figure out how many miles it was from one town to another by looking at the __________ on the map.

17. Did that new television come with a user's __________?

18. We found encyclopedias, dictionaries, and other __________ on the fourth floor of the library.

19. Darrell goes to visit Mr. John because Mr. John is a reliable __________ of information.

Check your answers on page 105

Reading Skills Review

Exercise 11

1. If you wanted to find a book about home repairs and you knew the author's name, how would you find where it is located in the library?

2. Suppose someone told you the title and subject of a magazine article. How would you go about finding the article in the library?

3. Suppose you wanted to find information about doing your own repairs on your car. How would you look for this in the library card catalog?

4. Suppose you wanted to find information about buying life insurance. How would you look for this in the library card catalog?

Check your answers on page 105

Exercise 12

READERS' GUIDE TO PERIODICAL LITERATURE

AUTOMOBILES—Export-import trade—*Continued*
Buying time [Japanese import controls] S. Blotnick. il Forbes 126:132+ D 8 '80
Foreign auto makers strike back at Detroit. J. L. Sheler. il U.S. News 89:75+ N 10 '80
Japanese imports in Europe. P Frere. Road & Track 32:77 D '80
Japan's rebuff to a Common Market pact. Bus W p60 D 1 '80
No to curbs on Japanese cars [ruling by U.S. International Trade Commission] il Time 116:86 N 24 '80
Protect us, O Lord, from protective tariffs. P. Bedar. il Car & Dr 26:18+ O '80
Slippery roads: Japanese autos invade Europe. il Time 117:65 Ja 12 81
Tiffs on trade [U.A.W. push for new quotas and tariff barriers to block Japanese imports] il Time 116:77 O 20 '80
Two faces of Ford. S. Chapman. New Repub 183:17-19 D 20 '80
U.A.W. on U.S. trade policy [address, October 20, 1980] D.F. Ephlin. Vital Speeches 47:145-8 D 15 '80
World automotive industry at a crossroads [address, October 14, 1980] C. K. Orski. Vital Speeches 47:89-93 N 15 '80
World trade [address, Octrober 20, 1980] R. B. Smith. Vital Speeches 47:130-3 D 15 '80

Fuel consumption

Driving down the high cost of gas. A. Arnott. il Redbook 155:49 O '80

History

American as all hell [1964-1968 Ford Mustang] il Time 116:92 D 1 '80
Fordor then and now [1940 Fordor Ford Delux] W. Weith. il Car & Dr 26:28 N '80
Retrospect:
1936 Packard 120 Convertible. L. Frank. il Motor T 32:89-93 O '80
Oldsmobile LA38 convertible coupe S. Grayson. il Motor T 32:114-15+ N '80

Laws and Regulations

See also
Automobiles, Foreign—Standards
By his deals you should know him. P. Bedard. il Car & Dr 26:20 N '80
Men who would be President [views of candidates on automotive issues] P. Bedard. il pors Car & Dr 26:55-6+ N '80
Update: life in all lanes. J. Tomerlin. Road & Track 32:146-7 D '80
Update: traffic safety and highway legislation news. J. Tomerlin. Road & Track 32:80-1 N '80
Vote for your car. L. Mandel. Motor T 32:72-5+ N '80

Leakage

Plugging those water leaks. P. Weissler. il Mech Illus 76:90+ S '80

Leasing and renting

Best ways to rent a car overseas. H. Geiseking. Trav/Holiday 154:95-6 O '80
Getting the best car-rental deal. P. Bohr. il Money 9:141-2+ N '80

Maintenance and repair

Auto ABCs:
Changing a flat. D. Chaikin. il Mech Illus 76:23-4+ O '80
How to replace wiper blades. D. Chaikin. il Mech Illus 76:46-7 D '80
Right way to use hand tools [automobile tools] D. Chaikin. il Mech Illus 77:28+ Ja '81
Simple steps to a cleaner running engine. D. Chaikin. il Mech Illus 76:37-8 S '80
Auto mail [questions and answers] P. Weissler. Mech Illus 76:14 S; 18 O; 21 N; 38 D '80
Automotive trouble-shooting quiz [cont] R. Hill. il Pop Sci 216:146+ F; 164+ My; 217:126-30 Jl;138-40 S '80 218:118-20 Ja '81
Clip-and-save guide to basic car maintenance: you can do it yourself! D. McCluggage. il Glamour 78:107-10 N '80
Emergency kit for your car. il Fam Handy 30:80+ D '80
50 plus challenge to highway officials [Road Ranger program helps stranded motorists in California] R. Hamilton. il 50 Plus 20:80 O '80
Frequency-of-repair records for 1974-1979 automobiles. il Consumer Rep 45:378-98 D '80
Guide to car care that can save you money. C. Berman. il Good H 192:161 Ja '81
How to keep your car new [special section] P. Weissler and D. Chaikin. il Mech Illus 76:53-69+ N '80
Popular mechanics fall 1980 car care guide [special section] il Pop Mech 154:123+ O '80
Repair ripoffs. F. M. H. Gregory. il Motor T 32:94-5 O '80
Ripoffs in auto repairs — any safeguards in sight? il U.S. News 89:64-5 D 1 '80
Smart things to do when your car goes in for repairs. Changing T 34:60 Ag '80
Winter driving [excerpt from Keeping warm] G. Olson. il Blair & Ketchums 7:78-86 D '80

Pollution control devices

Servicing the EGR systems of GM, Japanese and Volkswagen cars. M. Schultz. il Pop Mech 154: 35-8 D '80

Prices

Detroit vows to stay with its price policy. il Bus W p27-9 D 15 '80
Detroit's high-price strategy could backfire. il Bus W p 190+ N 24 '80
Iacocca has words for Washington [Chrysler interest rebates] Newsweek 96:78 D 15 '80
1981 car prices — how high is up? J. MacQueen. il Motor T 33:82-5 Ja '81

Purchasing

Buying a new car. Consumer Rep 45:361-6 D '80
How to drive a hard bargain buying a new car. D. H. Dunn. Bus W p 121-2 Ja 26 '81
On the road. J. Guthrie. por Work Wom 5:36+ D '80
Stretching your new-car dollar. B. Nagy. il Motor T 32:61-4 O '80
25 ways to avoid a lemon. F. M. H. Gregory. il Motor T 32:79-85 O '80

Recall

Auto recalls: how to know if you're an endangered driver. L. Borgeson. Vogue 170:106 N '80

Safety devices and and measures

Auto crash tests unsettle Japan and Detroit [views on auto safety design of J. Claybrook] R. J. Smith. il por Science 211:150-2 Ja 9 '81
Car seats that care for kids. P. Tai. il Money 9:115 D '80
Editor's report [seat belts and the 55 mph speed limit] J. Dianna. Motor T 32:8 N '80
Small cars: energy conservation at the price of safety? il Consumers Res Mag 63:16-20 N '80

Security measures

Auto antitheft devices. Consumer Rep 45:416-20 D '80
Auto theft: do you invite it? L. Borgeson, Vogue 170:169 O '80

1. If you wanted information about car mechanics who overcharge for repairs, what three magazine articles would you request?

2. On what pages of the magazines do these articles appear?

3. Fill out the periodical request forms for these magazines.

PERIODICAL REQUEST FORM

Name of periodical:

Dates wanted:

Your name:

PERIODICAL REQUEST FORM

Name of periodical:

Dates wanted:

Your name:

PERIODICAL REQUEST FORM

Name of Periodical:

Dates wanted:

Your name:

Check your answers on page 106

Exercise 13

1— What's Happening to Americans 1
How life is changing in the United States; economic and living conditions; comparison of conditions in 50 cities and states.

2— Individual Rights 16
How individual rights are changing; rights of women, minorities, disabled, consumers, and elderly; right to privacy and information; marriage and divorce laws.

1. What part of a book is this?

2. Where in the book would you expect to find this table?

3. On what page does chapter 7 begin?

4. Beginning on what page would you find information about unnecessary surgery?

5. Beginning on what page would you be most likely to find information about removing stains from furniture?

6. Beginning on what page would you be most likely to find information about forming a citizen group?

7. Beginning on what page would you be most likely to find information about the rights of a person who has been threatened with eviction from his home?

Check your answers on page 106

Exercise 14

1. What part of a book is this from?

2. Where in the book would you expect to find this table?

3. On what page would you find information about the proper containers for storing gasoline?

4. On what pages would you be most likely to find a list of hazardous products?

5. Suppose your doctor told you to stay away from foods that contain sodium. On what pages would you find information about the amount of sodium in certain foods?

6. Where in the book would you look to find information about services for the handicapped?

Check your answers on page 106

TV SCRIPTS—"More Pages"

ACT I
"The Word Is ..."

Open on Darrell leafing through a book in the stacks at the library. He is somewhat distracted; he keeps looking over at the librarian's desk, where an attractive young librarian is sitting. Finally he approaches her with the book.

DARRELL: Excuse me, miss, but could you tell me what this word means? Extra-ter-rest-rial?

LIBRARIAN: See that big book over there across the room? That's a dictionary—why don't you just go look it up? Didn't you tell me the other day that you're conducting some kind of investigation?

DARRELL: Yeah, that's right.

LIBRARIAN: Well, try investigating the dictionary!

DARRELL: But that's such a big book—I don't have time to look through all of that.

LIBRARIAN: You don't have to read it all. You look for the word you are investigating.

DARRELL: But there are so many words in there. There must be a zillion of 'em.

LIBRARIAN: Not quite a zillion. Estimates vary on the number of words in the English language. *The Guinness Book of World Records* says there are about 490,000 words.

DARRELL: That's still too many to know.

She softens her attitude a little; she gets up and leads him to the dictionary.

LIBRARIAN: Most people don't even know a tenth of all the words. The experts say an average person might know between 5,000 and 10,000 words, while a well-educated person might know 20,000 to 50,000 words.

DARRELL: I guess I'm in the second category!

LIBRARIAN: You mean you're "erudite"?

DARRELL: What did you call me?

LIBRARIAN: Relax—it means "smart." But if you're so smart, how come you don't know what "extraterrestrial" means?

She opens dictionary to find the word.

DARRELL: I guess it's one that slipped by me …

LIBRARIAN: What's that say?

He reads.

DARRELL: "Extraterrestrial: originating, located, or occurring outside the earth or its atmosphere." Hmmm, like in outer-space, huh?

LIBRARIAN: Correct. If you looked up the word "terrestrial," you'd find that it comes from the Latin word *terra*, which means "earth."

DARRELL: Very interesting.

LIBRARIAN: So now you know 50,000 and one words.

DARRELL: Aw, I really don't know that many words in the dictionary. I know a lot of street words, though.

LIBRARIAN: You know, they even have a dictionary of street words now.

She goes to a nearby shelf and produces the book.

LIBRARIAN: It's called *The Dictionary of American Slang*. According to it, the most frequently used words in the English language are "and," "be," "have," "it," "of," "the," "to," "will," and "you."

DARRELL: Yeah, I know people that talk like that! Add a few other words like "me" and "cool" and "eat" and that's about their whole vocabulary.

LIBRARIAN: Those aren't very interesting words, are they? They just happen to be the ones people use all the time. I'll show you one more book and then I have to get back to work.

She plucks another book off the shelf.

LIBRARIAN: This book is called *The Book of Lists*, and two of the lists in here give the most beautiful words and the worst-sounding words in the English language.

DARRELL: Is your name on the list of the most beautiful words?

She reads from the list.

LIBRARIAN: No, unless my name were Dawn or Lullaby or Melody or Mist or Tranquil.

DARRELL: What are some of the worst-sounding words?

LIBRARIAN: Let's see: Crunch… Gripe… Plump… Treachery… Flatulent… Phlegmatic… Jazz…

DARRELL: Jazz? What? Haven't they heard of Freddie Hubbard, or Chick Corea? Or McCoy Tyner?

LIBRARIAN: Well, you have to understand where this list came from. It says here it came from a 1946 meeting of a bunch of speech teachers, and to them jazz was strange; they didn't understand it. In fact, I bet they were scared of it, probably because it seemed so new and wild.

DARRELL: Aw, man, those cats didn't know nothing!

LIBRARIAN: You might say they weren't hip to the fact that jazz is the most creative sound being laid down. They were not enlightened by the knowledge that jazz is the cutting edge, the free-est of the free and the new-est of the new!

DARRELL: All right! I'm hip! Man, you don't need a dictionary to talk that talk.

LIBRARIAN: Jazz is my favorite kind of music. I'm into Coltrane, Thelonius Monk, Charlie Parker—some of the older dudes. But look, I have to get back to work now.

DARRELL: Uh, listen, why don't we get together some time and groove to some music?

She starts away.

LIBRARIAN: You'd have to ask my boyfriend about that, and he's really big, so I wouldn't recommend it!

DARRELL: Okay, if you say so.… Thanks for helping me with these words.

Fade out.

ACT II
"Oil's Well"

Open on Rhonda and Sherrylee in the driveway, approaching the car Rhonda bought. Rhonda has a box in which she has several quarts of oil, an oil filter, and a couple of wrenches; Sherrylee is carrying a pail.

Sound up as Sherrylee is talking.

SHERRYLEE: Why do you put oil in it, Momma?

RHONDA: So all the metal parts stay greased up—a lot of 'em rub together, and without oil they'd rust and jam up. Then your car wouldn't work. It's sorta like the Tin Man in *The Wizard of Oz*. You remember how he had to have his oil can or his arms and legs would rust and he couldn't move them?

SHERRYLEE: Yup.

RHONDA: Well, I'm gonna do the same thing here. Or at least, I think I am. I've never changed the oil in a car before. But I have this book that Candy gave me....

Throughout this sequence we will see Rhonda read a few instructions and then we'll see fast-motion footage of her following the instructions; for instance, after she reads "start engine," etc., we see her jump in the car and start it.

RHONDA: Lemme read what it says again. Or maybe I'll read a little and then do a little. "Park on a level place"—I've already done that. "Start engine and let it warm up. Turn off engine. Open hood and loosen oil filler cap. Place bucket or pan under oil drain plug and loosen plug."

Fast-motion stops after Rhonda gets under the car and puts a wrench on the drain plug; she has a hard time loosening the plug.

RHONDA: I can't get this drain plug thing to budge.

She hits the wrench with her hand and pulls on it some more; finally, it starts to give.

RHONDA: Uuuuh, there it goes! I think I've got it!

Her look of delight at loosening the plug quickly fades when the oil starts dripping down—on her head! We see it in slow-motion.

RHONDA: Ooooooooh! Darn it all!

She gets out of the way. Sherrylee giggles when she sees her mother with oil on her face.

RHONDA: You quit that laughing—it's just a little bit of oil; it's no big deal. Now then ...

She wipes her face.

RHONDA: "When oil has drained, replace plug and tighten."

She does so, again in fast-motion.

RHONDA: "Next, change oil filter. Use oil filter wrench if too tight to turn by hand. With clean cloth, wipe lip of area on engine which oil filter will cover. Screw on new filter by hand. When it touches the engine, turn it two-thirds of a turn more." Okay. "Refill with oil and put the filler cap back on." The man at the gas station said this old car would take about five quarts. "Start engine and check around drain plug and oil filter for leaks. If there is a leak, you haven't tightened either the plug or the filter enough. Run engine for a while, then turn it off and check the oil level. If necessary, add more oil."

She finishes checking the oil level by pulling out the dipstick.

RHONDA: What do you know! It worked! Sherrylee, we did it. Sherrylee, where are you?

She goes around to the other side of the car to find Sherrylee playing with the bucket of dirty oil; she has rubbed it on her elbows and knees.

RHONDA: Oh no. You did it! Why in tarnation ...?

SHERRYLEE: Just like the Tin Man, momma.

RHONDA: Oh no!

Fade out on Rhonda's exasperated expression.

ACT III
"Parent Liberation?"

Open on tight shot of Sherrylee's face. She is giving her undivided attention to something; camera pulls back to reveal that she is watching TV.

TV VOICE: Do what I tell you to do!

2ND TV VOICE (a child's voice): No! You're nuthin' but a turkey!

The last remark is greeted by loud, canned laughter, then applause, then theme music.

TV ANNOUNCER'S VOICE: Join us again tomorrow for another episode of *Mother's Little Monsters.*

Rhonda is nearby, fixing supper in the kitchen.

RHONDA: Okay, Sherrylee, that's enough TV for this afternoon.

You've watched two solid hours. Turn it off and play with your toys, or read one of your books for a while until dinner's ready.

Sherrylee gets up and walks over to Rhonda.

SHERRYLEE: No!

Rhonda raises an eyebrow.

RHONDA: Don't talk back to me, young lady.

SHERRYLEE: You're nuthin' but a turkey.

Rhonda's eyes almost bug out of her head.

RHONDA: What did you say to me?

Sherrylee suddenly loses some of her confidence, but repeats herself anyway.

SHERRYLEE: You're nuthin' but a turkey.

Rhonda grabs Sherrylee, turns her around, and gives her a spank; Sherrylee howls; Rhonda hollers.

RHONDA: Don't you ever talk to your Momma like that again! I'm gonna put you in your room and you're gonna stay there. I can't believe it! How can you talk like that? I know how—it's that darned TV! You got it straight off that TV. Maybe I'll just have to get rid of the TV, if that's what it teaches you!

Rhonda carries Sherrylee to her room and puts her on her bed; Sherrylee continues to cry.

SHERRYLEE *(wailing)*: Mommy, no ...

RHONDA: I'm gonna pull the plug for good! I'll teach you what happens in real life to "Mommy's little monster"!

Rhonda slams the door; her eyes are wide with anger. She stands with her back to the door, breathing hard from yelling; we hear Rhonda thinking to herself.

RHONDA (voice-over): I can't believe it! How could she be so disrespectful to me? Haven't I been a good mother? Of course I have. ... But maybe I shouldn't have spanked her. It makes me feel awful. Now I see what Daddy meant when he used to say, "This hurts me as much as you." But why should I feel guilty when she's acting like a brat? I didn't think I'd ever have trouble with her misbehaving.

Rhonda walks to a chair and sits; she looks confused, puzzled.

RHONDA: I thought that was something other people's kids do. ... There must be something I'm doing wrong. Some of those mothers down at the day care center say they never spank their kids, 'cause they don't want their kids to hate them. But their kids are the absolute worst! Will Sherrylee hate me because I spank her? … I never thought I'd be as strict as Momma and Daddy were with me; I always thought they overdid it. Am I overdoing it?

Begin gradual fade-out.

RHONDA: But I'm supposed to be mother and father, too. I have to teach her to respect me. But how—what do I do?

Fade completed.

Fade in on Rhonda's adult ed class; class members have just finished moving their chairs into a rough circle.

ANNE (the teacher): Well, what do you people want to talk about during today's discussion period?

A couple of people mumble something, but no one really answers.

ANNE: All right, tell you what. Tell me about some problem you're having that might be solved by reading something. Then we'll talk about where we'd look to find information about whatever it is that's bugging you. Like a health problem, something like that.

No one ventures forth.

SOMEONE *(jokingly)*: How 'bout a "wealth" problem!

ANNE: There's one we all have. But I doubt if we can solve that one very easily. We'd have to do a whole lot of reading! Years' worth, probably. How about a problem that's a little easier to solve?

Rhonda is timid, but she speaks anyway.

RHONDA: Well, I have one, but it's not any easier to figure out. How do you know if you're doing the right things when you raise a kid? I mean, are there some books that'll tell you what to do?

ANNE: Are there ever! That's the problem—there are so many books on a topic like that, all telling you different things, that it's easy to wind up even more confused than you were when you started. But the problems of parenthood is certainly a subject you can read about.

Another woman in the class speaks up.

NOREEN: I read somewhere that if you spank your kids you could scar them for life.

Laughter.

WALTER: Depends on how hard you spank 'em!

NOREEN: No, I mean scar them in an emotional way—make them hate you and not want to be with you. Do you think that's true?

ANNE: I don't know. That's one opinion. It's part of what's called the "permissive theory" of child-raising. It has been popular for the past 20 to 30 years. "Permissive" parents let their kids do what they want because they think too much discipline can prevent a child from growing up to be an individual: someone with a mind of their own. It's like giving a horse a loose rein, because you trust the horse to go the right way.

RHONDA: Shoot, if I give my little girl a loose rein, she'll become just like one of those spoiled brats you see on TV.

ANNE: Someone who believed in being a permissive parent would say that it's normal for children to get angry at their parents, and that it's normal for kids to rebel and not want to do what their parents tell them.

WALTER: That's a bunch of bull! If I didn't keep my 6-year-old in line, he'd bust the house apart. Kids need to know somebody's in charge.

ANNE: I just read a book that said basically the same thing. It was called *Parent Liberation*, and it said the permissive era is over. More parents are once again asserting their authority over their children, like our parents did—that's what this book said, anyway.

Class members groan: "Oh, no."

ANNE: The woman that wrote it said she called the book *Parent Liberation* because she wants to free parents from worrying too much about their children and from feeling guilty when they discipline their children. She said kids need the discipline.

NOREEN: I think I'm with her. I guess you've got to be firm with them, even if it means whupping their little hides.

ANNE: But there are ways of punishing them without spanking them. Or locking them in their rooms. Too much of either of those tactics might have negative results. In other words, spanking them and shutting them in their rooms aren't what you'd call "positive" experiences for the kid, you know what I mean? Negative punishment probably breeds resentment and anger in the kids.

Rhonda is perplexed.

RHONDA: So which book do you believe? Which theory, or whatever you call it, is the right one to choose? If you believed the wrong book, you might make some bad mistakes!

ANNE: All of them. And none of them. Books can give you a lot of information, some of it about fixing things like the kitchen sink. But all the books in the library can't tell you how to take care of some things. Some problems—like "How should I raise my kid?"—are too complex to answer. The problems we have with our kids, with each other—they're not like the ones solved in science books. Because we can fly a man to the moon, it doesn't mean we can make a marriage work or raise healthy, well-adjusted children. Raising kids isn't like baking a cake—there's no recipe to follow. People and their kids, all of us are so different from each other, one theory—or recipe—won't work for all of us.

RHONDA: Then it's not worth reading about all those different theories. I'd just get more confused.

ANNE: But by reading about how different people raise their kids, you do get a lot of ideas. It's like talking to someone about it, in a way. You learn different approaches. But just remember, all the experts in the world can't do it for you. It has to come from inside here.

Anne points to her heart.

Fade out.

ACT IV
"The 'Investigation' Continues"

Open on Darrell and a friend, Preston, walking down the street. They reach a street corner and pause; they look very serious.

PRESTON: Look, I gotta head this way …

DARRELL: All right, Preston. I'm really sorry to hear about your baby brother, man. It sounds bad. What did you say the disease is called?

PRESTON: Sickle-cell anemia. It has something to do with the blood.

DARRELL: And how did your brother get this stuff?

PRESTON: The doctors said it was hereditary, but I'm not sure what that means exactly. All I know is it's a disease that affects a lot of black children. Black people get it a lot more than white people do. And there's not much the doctors can do about it.… I gotta go, man. Be seeing you.

Preston heads in one direction …

DARRELL: Okay, Preston. I hope he gets better.

... Darrell heads in another and starts talking to himself.

DARRELL: Hmmm, it affects a lot of black children. I wonder if Gloria and Martin have heard about this? I wonder if little Oliver could get it?

Darrell stops walking and stands still.

DARRELL: Seems like I remember Gloria being kind of sick one time. They said she was anemic. I wonder if that has anything to do with it?

Darrell turns around and starts walking quickly.

DARRELL: Sounds like I better do another investigation.

Darrell turns a corner and the library appears.

DARRELL: Two weeks ago, I didn't know what this place was. Now I'm a regular customer.

Darrell walks up to the door and enters.

DARRELL: That's how it goes when you're in the "investigation" business.

First he goes to the dictionary; he thumbs through the S's and finds what he's looking for.

DARRELL: Here it is. "Sickle-cell anemia: a hereditary disease that causes clogged circulation of the blood; it can retard growth and lower resistance to infection; it can cause severe pain and lead to blindness, paralysis, or loss of speech; victims of the disease have too many abnormal red blood cells; it strikes about one of every 500 black children; Hispanics, Italians and Greeks are also prone to the disease." I wonder what "hereditary" means?

Turns through the dictionary to find "hereditary"; he reads the definition and then looks up with a worried look on his face; he gets up and heads for another part of the library.

DARRELL *(to himself again)*: I better see what's been written about this disease lately.

We see him reach for a volume of The Readers' Guide to Periodical Literature.

Fade out.

Fade in on Darrell coming into the apartment, where he finds Gloria and Martin and Oliver.

DARRELL: Gloria, Martin! Have you heard about this disease, sickle-cell anemia? I just heard about it, so I went and checked into it, 'cause it affects black kids like Oliver. I need to know one thing: Has anyone in our family, or in yours, Martin, ever had sickle-cell anemia?

GLORIA: No, I don't think so.

MARTIN: I never have heard of any in my family—why?

Darrell looks relieved.

DARRELL: Whew! I'm glad to hear that. Because it's a hereditary disease; if you get it, you inherit it from somebody in your family. Gloria, what about that time you were anemic?

GLORIA: That's a different sort of thing, I think.

DARRELL: Good. I'm glad I don't have to continue my investigation. I did find out some things so I can tell my friend Preston. His baby brother has it. Some scientists think they have a cure, something to do with the amount of water in the blood, but it may take a couple of years to test the cure.

GLORIA: I'm sorry to hear about your friend's brother. I've heard about sickle-cell anemia before, but I've never known anyone who had it.

DARRELL: I read about it in a recent issue of *Sepia*. There are about a quarter million black Americans with it. In Africa, there are about 10 million people with sickle-cell anemia.

MARTIN: You're getting pretty good at this investigating business, Darrell. You've been investigating one thing after another.

DARRELL: It's all a part of the ongoing, everyday investigation—the Big Investigation, if you know what I mean. You just gotta find out. I'm gonna try to call Preston to tell him what I read.

Darrell gives Oliver a soul shake on his way to the phone.

DARRELL: All right, Big O! Whatcha know?

Fade out.

Answers and Explanations

1st Intermission

1. Darrell wants to learn more about UFOs because he thinks that if he knows a lot about them, a UFO will come back to Earth and pick him up.
2. Mr. John says Darrell should start his investigation in the library.
3. Mr. John tells Darrell to go to the librarian for help.
4. Mr. John lists these sources of information:

(a) encyclopedia
(b) card catalog
(c) *Reader's Guide to Periodical Literature*

5. Rhonda tells her mother that a repair manual has helped her learn how to fix her car.
6. The directions Rhonda's mother gives Rhonda are incomplete. Rhonda's mother does not know what highway to take to get to her house.
7. If Rhonda tried to get to her mother's without using a map, Rhonda would probably get lost.
8. Rhonda tells her mother she will get a map.

Exercise 1

1. Cakes, Cereals, Cookies, Fruits, Meat, Poultry, Salads, Sauces, Shellfish, Vegetables

Exercise 2

1. *Crossword* should go between *Business* and *Editorials*.
2. *Movies* should go between *Living* and *Music*.
3. *Sports* should go between *Society* and *Theater*.

Exercise 3

1. *Fiction* falls between *fettle* and *fiddled*. Thus, the definition of *fiction* would be found on page 312.
2. *Fiat* falls between *fettle* and *fiddled*. Thus, the definition of the word *fiat* would be found on page 312.
3. *Femur* falls between *fellow* and *ferret*. Thus, the definition of the word *femur* would be found on page 310.
4. *Federalize* falls between *federalist* and *fellow*. Thus, the definition of *federalize* would be found on page 309.
5. *Festoon* falls between *ferret* and *fetter*. Thus, the definition of *festoon* would be found on page 311.
6. *Ferment* falls between *fellow* and *ferret*. Thus, the definition of *ferment* would be found on page 310.

Exercise 4

1. *Lawson* falls between *Lawrence* and *Lazarus*. Thus, the telephone number of a person named Lawson would be found on page 538.
2. *Leahy* falls between *Lazarus* and *Lebovic*. Thus, the telephone number of a person named Leahy would be found on page 539.

3. *Lau* falls between *Lating* and *Lauro*. Thus, the telephone number of a person named Lau would fall on page 536.
4. *Lasky* would be listed somewhere before *Latting*. Thus, from the information given, you cannot tell on what page the telephone number of a person named Lasky would be found.
5. *Lawn* falls between *Lauro* and *Lawrence*. Thus, the telephone number of a person named Lawn would be found on page 537.
6. *Laurence* falls between *Latting* and *Lauro*. Thus, the telephone number of a person named Laurence would be found on page 536.

Exercise 5

1. F. Grape juice is a beverage.
2. A. A skirt is part of a woman's wardrobe. Thus, it can be classified as women's apparel.
3. E. A carburetor is an automobile part.
4. C. An animal cage is a pet supply.
5. D. A neon sign is a type of sign.
6. B. Since a soap dish often is found in a bathroom, it can be classified as a bathroom accessory.

Exercise 6

1. *Hats* should go between *Furniture* and *Lingerie*.
2. *Jewelry* should go between *Furniture* and *Lingerie*.
3. *Hardware* should go between *Furniture* and *Lingerie*.
4. An eggbeater is used in cooking. Thus, it would be found in the *Cooking Equipment* department, which is on the third floor.
5. A necktie is worn by a man. Thus, it would be found in the *Menswear* department, which is on the first floor.
6. A hair dryer is a small appliance. Thus, it would be found on the fifth floor.
7. A sofa is a piece of furniture. Thus, it would be found on the seventh floor.
8. A dictionary is a book. Thus, it would be found on the sixth floor.

2nd Intermission

Exercise 7

1. The definition of the word *consumer* would be found in the dictionary.
2. To find magazine articles in the library, you must look in *The Readers' Guide to Periodical Literature.*
3. The titles of the chapters in a book are listed in the book's table of contents.
4. The entry is from an encyclopedia. It is a short article about a particular topic.
5. The part of a map that explains what the symbols on the map mean is called the legend.
6. A world atlas is a collection of maps of continents and countries.
7. The bibliography of a book lists other books that deal with the same subject.
8. The index of a book lists the page numbers on which specific topics are discussed.
9. The glossary of a book lists the definitions of terms used in the book.
10. If you don't know the name of a particular car mechanic, you would look in the yellow pages of a telephone directory under Automobile Repair and Service.
11. A cookbook is a collection of recipes.
12. The entry is from a dictionary. A dictionary gives, among other things, the definition of the word.
13. This is a sample from an index. An index gives the page numbers on which specific topics are discussed.
14. The entry is from the white pages of a telephone directory. The white pages list the addresses and telephone numbers of particular persons and places of business.
15. The entry is from a bibliography. A book's bibliography is a list of other books on the same subject.

Exercise 8

1. (c) A book that explains how to fix leaky faucets would fall under the general category HOME REPAIRS.
2. (c) The publisher of the book does not provide enough informa-

tion to find a book in the card catalogue. All of the other answer choices can be used to locate a book in the card catalogue.

3. (d) The card is a title card. The first line of the card is the book's title. Thus, the card would be filed under *G* for *Great*.
4. The call number of a book is needed so that either:
   - the librarian can get the book for you; or
   - you can locate the book in the library.

Exercise 9

1. This is a table of contents. A table of contents lists the chapters of a book in the order in which they appear.
2. Information about flat-rate manuals would be found in the second chapter, "The Plague of the Flat-Rate Manual." This chapter begins on page 12.
3. The book as a whole is about automobile repairs. You can guess that government regulations of auto repair shops probably are discussed in chapter 13, "Ask Not What Government Has Done For You …" This chapter begins on page 186.
4. The book as a whole is about automobile repairs. You can guess that the chapter of the book that discusses the price of auto parts is chapter 9, "Parts Problems." This chapter begins on page 134.

Exercise 10

1. This is an excerpt from an index. An index lists the page numbers of specific topics that are discussed in the book.
2. If you look under *C*, you will find that carpools are discussed on page 475.
3. If you look under *A*, you will find the entry for *Automobile.* The subheading *repairs* tells you that automobile repairs are discussed on pages 14-15, 47, and 485-487.
4. If you look under *C*, you will find the entry for *Children.* The subheading *television advertising* tells you this particular topic is discussed on pages 443-444.
5. If you look under *B*, you will find the entry for *Banking*. The subheading *loans* tells you that bank loans are discussed on pages 338-341.

After the Show

Vocabulary Review

1. *Enamel* is a paint that when dry has a glossy appearance.
2. A *phenomenon* is a fact or event that can be seen.
3. *Terms* are words used in a specific field.
4. A *UFO* is an unidentified flying object.
5. A *private eye* is a person who investigates crimes.
6. An *investigation* is a search for information.
7. A *category* is a general group or class.
8. *Exterior* means outside.
9. *Periodicals* are magazines and journals that are issued on a regular basis.
10. A *stimulant* is a substance that increases the rate of activity.
11. A *legend* on a map explains what the symbols on the map mean.
12. A *librarian* is a person who works in a library.
13. A *definition* is the meaning of a word.
14. *Coordinates* are a number and a letter that are used to locate a point on a map.
15. *Interior* means inside.
16. The *scale* on a map indicates units of measurement.
17. A *manual* is a small guide or instruction book.
18. *Reference* books are books that provide useful information.
19. A *source* is a book or person that supplies information.

Reading Skills Review

Exercise 11

1. If you know the author's name, the easiest way to locate a book is to look for the author card in the card catalog. To do this, you must look under the letter with which the author's last name begins. Once you find this card, the book's call number will help you locate the book.
2. To find a magazine article, you would look up the subject in the *Readers' Guide* and find the title in the alphabetical list under the subject. Then you would either fill out a periodical request form and give it to the librarian or look for the periodical on the shelves.
3. The easiest way would be to look for subject cards in the card catalog. The subject probably would be listed as *Automobiles—*

Maintenance and Repair.

4. The easiest way would be to look for subject cards in the card catalog. The subject probably would be listed as *Insurance*.

Exercise 12

1. First, look under the major heading *Automobiles*. Then, look under the subheading *Maintenance and Repair*. There you will find three magazine articles on the subject:
   (a) "Repair ripoffs"
   (b) "Ripoffs in auto repairs—any safeguard in sight?"
   (c) "Smart things to do when your car goes in for repairs."
2. (a) "Repair ripoffs" appears on pages 94-95.
   (b) "Ripoffs in auto repairs—any safeguard in sight?" appears on pages 64-65.
   (c) "Smart things to do when your car goes in for repairs" appears on page 60.
3. (a) Name of Periodical: Motor T.
   Dates wanted: October 1980
   (b) Name of Periodical: U.S. News
   Dates wanted: December 1, 1980
   (c) Name of Periodical: Changing T.
   Dates wanted: August 1980

Exercise 13

1. This is a table of contents. A table of contents lists the chapters of a book in the order in which they appear.
2. The table of contents usually is located in the front of the book.
3. Chapter 7 begins on page 172.
4. *Unnecessary surgery* is listed under chapter 10, "Health Care." This chapter begins on page 251.
5. *Stain removal methods* are listed under chapter 7, "Clothing and Furnishings." This chapter begins on page 172.
6. *Citizen groups* are listed under chapter 4, "Helping Yourself." This chapter begins on page 78.
7. *Tenant rights* are listed under chapter 6, "Housing and Land." This chapter begins on page 155.

Exercise 14

1. This is an excerpt from an index. An index is an alphabetical list of specific topics that are discussed in the book.
2. Indexes usually are found in the backs of books.

3. First look under the heading *Gasoline*. Then look under the subheading *cans*. This subheading tells you that gasoline cans are discussed on page 491.
4. The heading *Hazardous products* tells you this topic is discussed on pages 570-581.
5. First look under the heading *Food*. The subheading *sodium content* tells you this topic is discussed on pages 219-221.
6. Look under the heading *Handicapped*. There is a cross-reference to the heading *Disabled*. Thus, you would have to look under *D* for *Disabled* on another page of the index.

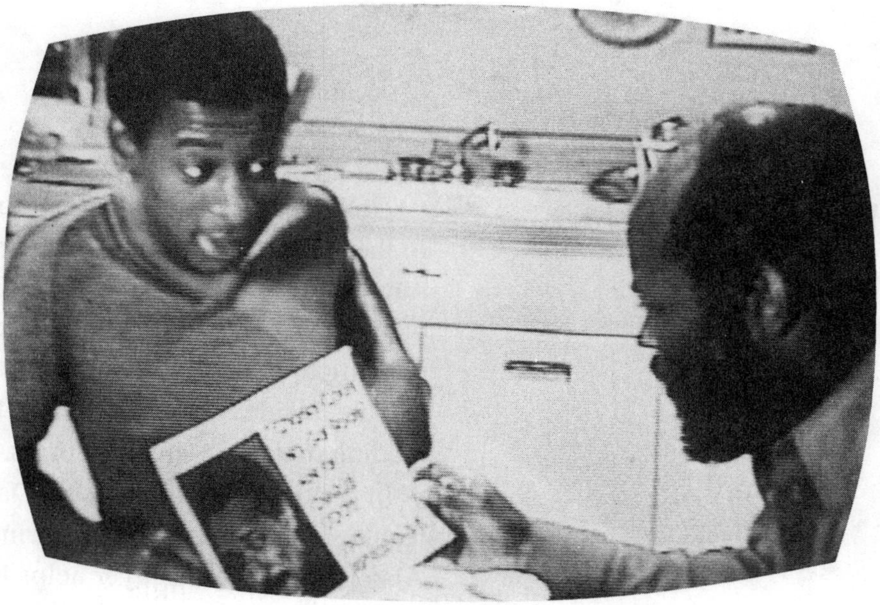

6

Understanding Forms

In this program, you will practice reading and filling out various parts of forms. You will see that while forms may differ, there are certain things that frequently appear on many different types of forms.

Videotape Preview

The videotape you are about to watch is divided into three parts. In the first part, Darrell wants to vote for an old friend who is running for state representative. Darrell asks Martin to help him fill out a voter registration form. Also in this part, Rhonda decides she is going to look into getting a credit card.

The "Inside Story" part of the tape discusses the various types of reading material found on forms.

In the third part of the tape, Darrell is disappointed in the election results but realizes that registering to vote was not a complete loss. Also in this part, a lawyer helps Rhonda apply for and get a department store credit card.

As you watch the first part of the tape, try to answer the following questions:

- What kind of form does Darrell have to fill out before he can vote for Charles Coots?
- According to Charles Coots, how often do you have to vote in order for your registration to remain valid?
- According to Martin, what choices does Darrell have for the "party affiliation" section of the form?
- Where does Martin tell Darrell to take the form after it has been filled out?
- How did Candy find out about Ruby Hatton?
- According to Candy, why does Ruby Hatton help women for free?

Vocabulary

The following words are used on the tape. Before you watch the tape or do any work in this lesson, study the meanings of these words:

anemic: suffering from an inadequate amount of red blood cells
*A person who is **anemic** usually is pale and weak.*

ally: a person or country that cooperates with another person or country
*During World War II, France was an **ally** of England and of the United States.*

applicant: one who applies for, or requests, something (for example, a loan or job)
*The **applicant** was told that his request for a loan had been approved.*

authorize: to officially approve or permit
*Is it true that a bank executive has to **authorize** a loan before the applicant can receive any money?*

cast one's ballot: to give in one's vote (literally, to hand in a piece of paper on which one's vote is written)

I ***cast my ballot*** *for the Democratic candidate even though I knew he had no chance of winning.*

comprehensive insurance: car insurance that covers losses caused by fire and theft

Many people get ***comprehensive insurance*** *because more and more cars are stolen each day.*

consent: to agree to something or to give one's permission

The doctor said he will not perform the surgery unless I ***consent*** *to it.*

creditor: a person or institution that lends money

Before they will lend you money, ***creditors*** *want to make sure you will be able to repay the loan.*

finance charge: a percentage of the amount you owe on your credit card account that is added to your bill on a regular basis

I decided to forget about getting a credit card because the ***finance charge*** *was too high.*

flier: a printed sheet of paper that is given out by hand

The candidate decided that the best way to make himself known was to hand out ***fliers****.*

invalid: not legally acceptable or usable

William's driver's license is ***invalid*** *because he has received too many speeding tickets.*

liability insurance: car insurance that covers you if you are at fault for injury to others or damage to property

The insurance salesman said ***liability insurance*** *covers the losses if a person in another car is hurt in an accident.*

outstanding: not yet paid or settled

The bank refused to give him a loan because he still has many bills ***outstanding****.*

party affiliation: the political party you support

If you fill in your ***party affiliation*** *when you register to vote, you* *can vote in that party's primary.*

platform: the positions a political candidate or party takes on the issues
*Part of the candidate's **platform** is that he supports arms limitation talks.*

polls: the place where one goes to vote
*In next week's election, people are expected to flock to the **polls** in record numbers.*

primary: an election among members of a political party to choose that party's candidate in a general election
*In a presidential election, the winner of the Democratic **primary** runs against the candidates of the other parties.*

register: to submit one's name for voting, school, etc.
*The League of Women Voters can tell you how you can **register** to vote.*

Watch Part 1

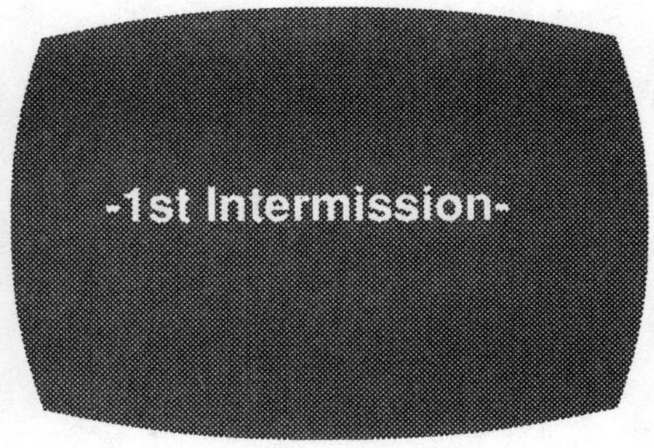

It seems that whenever you make an important decision—to look for a new job, to apply for credit, to open up a bank account—someone hands you a form to fill out.

Forms usually are time-consuming, and they often are complicated. But forms may not be as complicated as they appear to be at first. Forms may differ in some respects, but you will see that the same information appears again and again on many different types of forms. Once you know what to expect from a form, you will find that the form is easier to fill out.

The following questions are based on the situations on the tape:

1. What kind of form does Darrell have to fill out before he can vote for Charles Coots?

2. According to Charles Coots, how often do you have to vote in order for your registration to remain valid?
   (a) every year
   (b) every two years
   (c) every three years
   (d) every four years

3. According to Martin, what choices does Darrell have for the "party affiliation" section of the form?

4. According to Martin, why might Darrell want to register for Charles Coots's party?

5. Where does Martin tell Darrell to take the form after it has been filled out?
   (a) the post office
   (b) the polls
   (c) the courthouse
   (d) other people in the neighborhood

6. Why does Rhonda think it is unfair that the department store dropped her charge account after her divorce?

7. How did Candy find out about Ruby Hatton?
   (a) through an ad in the paper
   (b) from a friend
   (c) from the yellow pages
   (d) from the "Women's Help Line"

8. According to Candy, why does Ruby Hatton help women for free?

Check your answers on page 158

Before you fill out any form, it is important to keep the following tips in mind:

- Read all of the instructions that come with the form.
- Use a pen or a typewriter to fill out the form. Don't use a pencil unless the form asks you to. This is so the information you fill in will not be erased accidentally.
- Print all information. Make sure your writing can be read by someone other than you.
- Do not leave anything blank unless it does not apply to you. (Do not make any marks in a space that says "Do not write in this space" or "Office use only.")

You probably are aware that there are hundreds of different kinds of forms—forms for loans, forms for insurance, forms for medical services, etc. But all forms ask for two things:

- basic information about yourself
- additional information that depends on the form

Basic Information about Yourself

No matter what kind of form you are filling out, you probably will have to supply all of the following information:

Your Name: All forms ask for your name. But how they want you to fill in your name can differ. Some forms provide a line on which you are to fill in your name:

Name: ______________________________
First M.I. Last

("M.I." means middle initial—the first letter of your middle name.)

Name: ______________________________
First M.I. Last

Sometimes, you are asked to write your last name *before* your first name:

Name: ______________________________
Last First M.I.

Name: ______________________________
Last First M.I.

Some forms ask you to fill in your name in boxes. You must fill in one letter of your name in each box, leaving at least one empty box between your first name, last name, and middle initial:

NAME: FIRST INITIAL LAST

NAME: FIRST M A R Y INITIAL A LAST A L V A R E Z

LAST FIRST INITIAL

LAST A L V A R E Z FIRST M A R Y INITIAL A

Your Address: Most forms ask for your address. The format for your name—lines or boxes—usually is followed for your address. You need to include the number of your house or apartment building; the name of your street or rural route; your apartment number; your village, town, or city; your state (this can be abbreviated); and your zip code. (Occasionally, you also are asked to include the name of your county.)

Home address (Number and street or rural route)
City or town, State and ZIP code

Home address (Number and street or rural route) 147 Cooper Avenue Apt. 4B
City or town, State and ZIP code Hartsdale, Il. 21714

NO AND STREET		APT
CITY AND STATE		ZIP CODE

NO AND STREET	1 4 7 C O O P E R A V E N U E	APT 4 B
CITY AND STATE	H A R T S D A L E I L	ZIP CODE 2 1 7 1 4

On some forms, you may have to give an indication of how settled you are. These forms ask you to fill in how long you have lived at your present address. If you have not lived there for a certain amount of time, you may have to fill in your previous address.

NO AND STREET		APT.	HOW LONG YRS MOS
CITY AND STATE		ZIP CODE	
PREVIOUS ADDRESS (IF LESS THAN 2 YRS AT PRESENT)			

NO AND STREET	147 COOPER AVENUE	APT 4B	HOW LONG 1 YRS. 9 MOS
CITY AND STATE	HARTSDALE IL	ZIP CODE 21714	
PREVIOUS ADDRESS (IF LESS THAN 2 YRS AT PRESENT) 2135 Clove Drive, Richmond, N.J. 17632			

Your Telephone Number: Many forms ask you to fill in your telephone number. Parentheses—( )—usually are provided for your area code.

HOME TELEPHONE NUMBER

( )

HOME TELEPHONE NUMBER

( )

Your Social Security Number: Every working person in the United States must have a Social Security card and number. You can apply for a Social Security card and number at the local Social Security office or the post office. The Social Security number is a nine-digit number. On forms, you often must fill in your social security number in boxes.

SOCIAL SECURITY NUMBER
_ _ _ – _ _ – _ _ _ _

SOCIAL SECURITY NUMBER
189 – 35 – 6461

Your Date of Birth (Or Age): Many forms ask you to fill in your date of birth. Often, you must convert your date of birth into numbers. Then you must fill in these numbers in boxes or between slashes (/ /). In number form, your date of birth is:

(1) the number of the month (each month of the year has a number—January is 1, June is 6, December is 12)

(2) the day of the month (1, 12, 27)

(3) the last two digits of the year (1948–48, 1955–55)

DATE OF BIRTH: / /

DATE OF BIRTH: / /

Other forms simply ask you to fill in your age.

AGE:

AGE:

Your Sex: Either fill in or circle M for Male or F for Female.

SEX: SEX: M F

SEX: SEX: M F

Your Marital Status: Many forms ask you to check off your marital status: married, single, divorced, separated, or widowed. On other forms, you must fill in your marital status in a blank space. Still other forms give only married and single as choices,but these forms usually give instructions for people who are divorced, separated, or widowed.

Marital status: ☐ Single ☐ Married ☐ Divorced ☐ Separated ☐ Widowed

MARITAL STATUS

Marital status: ☐ Single ✓ Married ☐ Divorced ☐ Separated ☐ Widowed

MARITAL STATUS Separated

Marital Status:

☐ Single ☐ Married

(If divorced, separated, or widowed, check single)

Marital Status:

✓ Single ☐ Married

(If divorced, separated, or widowed, check single)

Your Signature and the Date: The last thing most forms ask you to do is to sign the form and fill in the date on which you completed the form. Since everyone's signature is different, your signature proves that you, and no one else, filled out (or at least approved) the information on the form. Thus, the form is not "official" until you sign it.

Signature ➤ .... Date ➤ ...., 19 ....

Signature ➤ .... Date ➤ ...., 19 ....

Exercise 1

1. What four tips should you keep in mind when filling out any form?

2. Your name is Joseph Louis Armstrong. How would you fill out the following section of a form?

NAME: | | | | | | | | | | | | | | | | | | | | | | | | | | | | | | |
Last First M.I.

3. Your date of birth is February 9, 1954. How would you fill out the following section of a form?

DATE OF BIRTH: / /

4. Your Social Security number is 217-45-8778. How would you fill out the following section of a form?

Social Security Number

| | | | – | | – | | | | |

5. Your address is 135 Harvest Drive, Glendale, WI 31425. How would you fill out the following section of a form?

ADDRESS: ______________________________
Number and Street

____
City or Town State Zip

6. Your telephone number is 323-4874. The area code is 545. How would you fill out the following section of a form?

TELEPHONE: (______) ________ - ____________

7. You recently have gotten a divorce. How would you fill out the following section of a form?

MARITAL STATUS: ______________________

8. Your date of birth is October 2, 1940. How would you fill out the following section of a form?

Date of Birth ☐☐☐☐☐☐

9. Your name is John Henry Edwards. How would you fill out the following section of a form?

NAME: ____________________________
Last First M.I.

10. You are a single man. How would you fill out the following section of a form?

Marital Status: ☐ Single	☐ Married	☐ Divorced	
	☐ Separated	☐ Widowed	
Sex: M F			

11. Your address is 3251 Richmond Avenue, Apartment 12A, Rockland, Connecticut 17435. You have lived there for 12 years. Your previous address was 13 Ludlow Street, Apartment 15, Brooklyn, New York 11023. How would you fill out the following section of a form?

HOME ADDRESS	NUMBER AND STREET			
	CITY	STATE	ZIP	YEARS THERE
PREVIOUS HOME ADDRESS (If less than 3 years at present address)	NUMBER AND STREET			
	CITY	STATE	ZIP	

12. Your husband died five years ago. You have not remarried. How would you fill out the following section of a form?

Marital Status: ☐ Single	☐ Married
(If separated, divorced, or widowed, check single.)	

13. Your Social Security number is 235-21-1245. How would you fill out the following section of a form?

SOCIAL SECURITY NUMBER: ______-______-__________

14. Your name is Marsha T. Walsh. You completed a form on January 14, 1980. How would you fill out the following section of the form?

SIGNATURE:____________________ DATE: _____/_____/_____

15. You are 35 years old. How would you fill out the following section of a form?

AGE

16. Your name is Thomas P. Evans. How would you fill out the following section of a form?

FIRST NAME MIDDLE INITIAL LAST NAME

17. Your address is 132 92nd Avenue, Apartment 3D, Dolton, MI 52435. How would you fill out the following section of a form?

NO. AND STREET		APT.
CITY AND STATE		ZIP CODE

18. Your address is 14 Adams Avenue, Apartment 5F, Highland, CA 91324. You have lived there for 3 years and 2 months. Your previous address was 32 Grant Road, Middletown, NJ 19678. How would you fill out the following section of a form?

ADDRESS: ______________________________
Number and Street Apt.

____
City State Zip

HOW LONG AT THIS ADDRESS? ____ yrs. ____ mos.

PREVIOUS ADDRESS: ______________________________

19. Your name is Robert Andrew Fodera. Your address is 85 Nelson Avenue, Northbrook, TX 84376. You were born on August 2, 1951. Your telephone number is area code 312, 558-8942. Your Social Security number is 215-48-7283. You are married. You are filling out this form on July 24, 1981. How would you fill out this section of the form?

NAME:	Last	First	M.I.
ADDRESS:	Number and Street		
	City, State, Zip		
PHONE: ( )		DATE OF BIRTH: / /	
SOCIAL SECURITY NUMBER:			
MARITAL STATUS:	☐ single	☐ married	☐ divorced
		☐ widowed	☐ separated
SIGNATURE:			DATE:

20. Your name is Daniel Charles Murphy. Your address is 453 Madison Avenue, Apartment 16, Watertown, FL 52364. You have lived there for 2 years and 6 months. Your previous address was 15 Morrison Street, Glen Ridge, NH 23785. Your telephone number is area code 786, 636-0905. Your Social Security number is 315-48-1252. You were born on March 31, 1948. You are legally separated. You are filling out this form on September 30, 1981. How would you fill out the following section of the form?

NAME	First	M.I.	Last		
NO. AND STREET					
CITY AND STATE		ZIP		HOW LONG:	
PREVIOUS ADDRESS (IF LESS THAN 3 YEARS AT PRESENT)					
PHONE: ( )		DATE OF BIRTH:			
SOCIAL SECURITY NO.:		MARITAL STATUS:			
SIGNATURE:				DATE:	

Check your answers on page 158

Watch Part 2:
"The Inside Story"

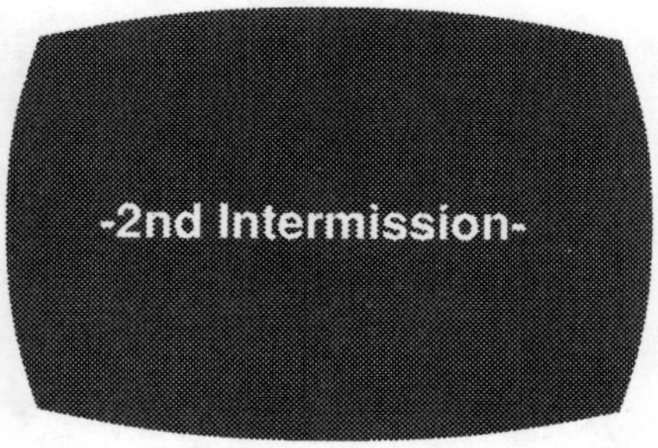

In addition to basic information about yourself, most forms ask for additional information. This information depends on the type of form it is. For example, an application for a loan will ask for financial information, and an application for a job will ask for information about your work experience.

But even in this part of a form, there are special sentences and passages that you will find again and again on many different types of forms. Here are some of these sentences and passages:

Affirmation: On many forms, just above the line for the signature, you will find a sentence or sentences like the following:

> Under penalty of perjury, I declare that I have examined this application, and to the best of my knowledge and belief, it is true, correct, and complete.

This type of statement is called an *affirmation statement*. Whenever you sign and hand in a form that contains an affirmation statement, you are in effect swearing that what you have written on the form is, as far as you know, true. If you deliberately lie on a form, you may be charged with perjury. Perjury is a crime in which one swears to something that is untrue.

You also may find a similar passage in this area of the form:

> WARNING: Any willful false statement may subject you to criminal penalty.

This also is an affirmation statement, but it is stated in stronger terms.

Conditions: Conditions are the terms, or demands, you must fulfill when you accept an offer. Conditions often are found on credit card applications (see the section on "Credit Terms" below). Conditions also are found on book or record club membership forms. Here's an example:

> Enclosed is my check for $1.00. Please send me the four books I have indicated below. I agree to purchase four selections within the next year at the regular club prices.

In this book club offer, the condition is that you will buy four books within a year at the regular club prices. (Check to see if there is any indication of what these "regular" prices are.) Also, book and record club forms often have statements like the following:

> Each month, you will receive a card describing that month's premium selection. If you would like the selection, do nothing. It will be shipped to you automatically. If you do not want the selection, return the card within 10 days.

What this means is that the book or record club will send you the monthly selection, whether you want it or not, unless you send in that card within 10 days of the time you receive it. If you forget to send in the card or if you are a little late, you're out of luck.

Always read conditions carefully. Remember, when you send in a form with conditions on it, it's like signing a contract. You are required to fulfill the conditions, or terms, of the offer.

Consent: To *consent* means to agree to or to give permission. You can find consent statements in financial and hospital forms. Here's an example of a consent statement from a loan application:

> I hereby authorize the County National Bank to investigate any of the financial information on this application. I authorize the County National Bank to investigate any credit references I have given or may hereafter give to the County National Bank. I also authorize the County National Bank to investigate any statement or other data obtained from any person pertaining to my credit or financial history.

In the first sentence of this consent statement, the applicant gives the bank permission to investigate whatever information the applicant wrote on the application.

In the second sentence, the applicant gives the bank permission to investigate the applicant's present or future credit references. A credit reference is a person or institution that can give information about the applicant's ability to repay debts.

In the third sentence, the applicant gives the bank pemission to investigate what others say about the applicant's ability to repay debts.

If you ever need surgery, you probably will have to fill out a hospital consent form. These forms reduce the chances that the surgeon will be sued for malpractice. Here's a paragraph from a hospital consent form:

> I, the undersigned, hereby authorize Dr. ____________ to perform the following operation:
>
> ____.
>
> I also authorize Dr. ________________ to perform whatever additional surgical procedures he considers therapeutically necessary during the course of the operation. I consent to the administration of whatever anesthetics Dr. ______________ deems necessary.

In the first sentence of this consent form, the patient gives the doctor permission to perform a specific operation. This is so the patient cannot sue the doctor for performing an operation the patient did not know about.

In the second sentence, the patient gives the doctor permission to perform whatever additional operations may be necessary during the course of the operation. Thus, the doctor does not have to awaken you to ask permission to perform another operation that may be needed to save your life. But this means that if the doctor performs an additional operation and anything goes wrong, all the doctor has to do is show why he thought the additional operation was necessary. You cannot sue him for performing an operation you did not approve.

In the third sentence, the patient gives the doctor permission to administer whatever anesthetics the doctor feels are necessary. Again, if anything goes wrong, all the doctor has to do is show why he thought the anesthetics were necessary.

You can see that consent statements can be very important. You also can see that consent statements can be complicated. You can recognize them by looking for words like *consent*, *authorize*, *agree*, *permit*, and *approve*. Remember, your consent is not given until you sign and hand in the form.

Credit Terms: Before you send in an application for a credit card or a loan, read the explanation of the terms, or demands, that you must fulfill. Here's an example from a credit card application:

> FINANCE CHARGE: The finance charge is figured by multiplying the Average Daily Balance shown on your monthly statement by the following monthly rates:
> - 1 1/2% on the first $500 (minimum finance charge—50¢)
> - 1% on the amount over $500
>
> PAYMENT: I agree to pay for all purchases made by me or by others who have my permission to use my account. I agree that each month I will pay at least:
> - 10% of my monthly balance up to $500; plus
> - 20% of the portion of this balance that is over $500

I understand that I may be required to pay all of my unpaid balance if I fail to make any required payment when it is due.

The first section of these terms explains how the finance charge is determined. The finance charge is the amount you must pay for the privilege of using the credit card. The "Average Daily Balance" is the average amount of money you owe from day to day for a given month. The finance charge is 1 1/2% of the first $500 of this amount plus 1% of the part of this amount that is more than $500. For example, if your balance were $600, the finance charge would be:

	1 1/2% of $500	= $7.50
+	1% of $600 - $500, or $100	= $1.00
	Finance charge	= $8.50

The next section of the terms explains how payments are to be made. The minimum you must pay is 10% of your average daily balance—including the finance charge—up to $500, plus 20% of the part of your monthly balance that is over $500. For example, if your Average Daily Balance were $700, your minimum payment would be:

	10% of $500	= $50
+	20% of $700 - $500, or $200	= $40
	Minimum payment	= $90

The last section of the terms explains that if you do not make a payment on time, you may have to pay your entire unpaid balance at once.

Terms differ from credit card to credit card. For some credit cards, you must pay the entire balance every month. For others, you pay a percentage of the unpaid balance each month. Also, finance charges differ from card to card. Be sure to read the terms carefully before you send in your application for a credit card.

Now, read the following passage from a loan application:

Interest on this loan is charged at the rate of 2 1/2% per month on any part of the unpaid balance not in excess of $100.00, 2% per month on any part of the unpaid balance in excess of $100.00 but not in excess of $900.00, and 1 1/4% per month on any remainder of the unpaid balance.

Suppose you were interested in taking out a loan for $1,100. According to these terms, your first interest charge would be:

2 1/2% on first $100	=	$2.50
2% on $300 - $100, or $200	=	$4.00
1 1/2% on $900 - $300, or $600	=	$9.00
1% on $1,100 - $900, or $200	=	$2.00
First monthly interest charge	=	$17.50

This would be computed each month until your loan was paid off. Interest charges for loans differ depending on who gives you the loan. Banks charge less interest than finance companies, but it is easier to get a loan from a finance company. Read the terms of the loan carefully before you decide to apply for one.

Disclaimer: A *disclaimer* is a denial of responsibility. A manufacturer who issues a warranty for a product almost always includes a disclaimer, or an explanation of the situations in which the warranty is invalid. Here's an example:

> This warranty does not apply to any Cardinal product damaged by accident, misuse, abuse, improper wiring, fire, acts of God, or any parts or service furnished by anyone other than Cardinal or one of its authorized dealers.

This disclaimer basically says that the warranty does not apply unless Cardinal, the manufacturer, causes the damage. (An act of God is something—such as a storm or an earthquake—over which humans have no control.) This is the cause with most disclaimers. But some disclaimers are more reasonable than others. Whenever you consider buying a product that comes with a warranty, make sure the disclaimer sounds fair and reasonable.

Employment: The most important form you have to fill out when you start a new job is the W-4 Form, or Employee's Withholding Allowance Certificate. Here's a passage from the form:

> If you have unusually large itemized deductions, you may claim the allowance(s) for itemized deductions to avoid having too much income tax withheld from your wages. On the other hand, if you and your spouse are both employed or you have more than one employer, you should take steps to assure that enough has been withheld. If you find that you need more withholding, claim fewer exemptions or ask for additional withholding.

To make it easier for you to pay your income taxes at the end of the year, the government takes money out of each of your paychecks. The amount taken out is determined by the number of allowances you claim on the W-4 Form. The more allowances you claim, the less money will be taken out of each paycheck.

But the amount taken out of your paychecks for one year is not the same as your income tax for that year. If the amount you have to pay for income tax is more than the amount taken out of your paychecks, you will have to pay the difference. If the amount you have to pay for income tax is less than the amount taken out of your paychecks, you will get a refund for the amount the government owes you.

Thus, claiming many allowances may result in more money on payday, but it also increases the chances that you will owe the government money at the end of the year. Claiming fewer allowances reduces your take-home pay but increases your chances of getting a refund at the end of the year. The passage from the W-4 Form explains that by adjusting the number of your allowances, you can make sure you will not have to pay too much at the end of the year. At the same time, you can make sure your take-home pay will be enough to cover your day-to-day expenses.

At the end of this lesson, you will find several complete forms on which you can practice filling out forms. If you would like more practice, the following forms are easy to find:

FORM	WHERE TO FIND IT
Automobile	
Application for a driver's license	Your local department of motor vehicles
Application for automobile insurance	Any insurance agent
Financial	
Bank forms (applications for checking and savings accounts, deposit and withdrawal slips, checks, check logs)	Any bank
Credit card application	Banks and retail stores
Income tax form	The Internal Revenue Service, the post office, or a tax return preparation company
Social Security application	Local Social Security office or the post office
Medical	
Application for health insurance	Any insurance agent
Health insurance claim form	Any insurance agent
Hospital admissions form	Any hospital
Other	
Job application	Any local business

Passage 1

The manufacturer is not responsible for damages caused by abuse, mishandling, neglect, accident, or fire. The manufacturer is not responsible for damages that result from service by anyone other than the manufacturer or an authorized dealer or service center. If damages result from a part or parts that are supplied by anyone other than the manufacturer or an authorized dealer or service center, the manufacturer shall not be held responsible for these damages.

1. On what kind of form would you be likely to find the above passage?

(a) book or record club form
(b) W-4 Form
(c) product warranty
(d) credit application

2. Under what conditions is this product not covered?

3. In order to make sure the coverage will remain in effect, where should you take the product if it has to be repaired?

4. Based on the information in the passage, you can infer that the product would be covered if
   (a) the owner of the product drops the product and damages it
   (b) the product is destroyed by fire
   (c) the manufacturer improperly installs a part
   (d) a friend tries to repair the product and damages it even more

Check your answers on page 161

Passage 2

I, ________________, hereby authorize the Bay City Savings and Loan Association to investigate my credit record. I also authorize the Bay City Savings and Loan Association to investigate the accuracy of any statement made on this application by me and to investigate any statements made by others, whether individuals or institutions, concerning my credit history.

1. On what type of form would you expect to find the above passage?
   (a) an application for a loan
   (b) an application for a job
   (c) a driver's license application
   (d) a product warranty

2. What do you think is to be filled in on the blank line in the first line of the passage?

3. In your own words, explain what the passage means.

Check your answers on page 162

Passage 3

You do not have to buy a minimum number of books per year. Just buy 4 books during your membership. After that you may cancel your membership at any time. Each month, you will be offered one or two main selections. In addition, from time to time you will be offered special selections (all selections are at our regular discount price). If you want the main or special selection(s), do nothing. You will receive them automatically. If you do not want any selection, mark the order form "no selection" and return it by the date specified on the card. You always have 10 days to decide. If you get an unwanted selection because you did not have 10 days to decide, return it at our expense.

1. According to the passage, how many books must you buy if you decide to accept this offer?
   (a) 1
   (b) 4
   (c) 12
   (d) you do not have to buy any books

2. According to the passage, what is the "regular discount price"?

3. According to the passage, what must you do if you want the monthly selection(s)?

4. According to the passage, what must you do if you do not want the monthly selection(s)?

5. According to the passage, how much time do you have to decide whether or not you want the monthly selection(s)?

6. Which of the following can be inferred from the information in the passage?
   (a) If you receive an unwanted selection at any time, you can return it at the company's expense.
   (b) If you forget to send in the card within 10 days and are sent an unwanted selection, you are stuck with the book.
   (c) If you do not want the monthly selection or the special selections, return these books within 10 days.
   (d) If you want the monthly selection or the special selections, return the card within 10 days.

Check your answers on page 162.

Passage 4

The following passage is from a job application:

> I declare that the statements made on all pages of this application are, to the best of my knowledge, true and complete. I understand that any false statement on this application may be considered sufficient grounds for dismissal.

1. Near what part of a form would you expect to find the above passage?
   (a) date of birth
   (b) address
   (c) signature
   (d) Social Security number

2. In your own words, explain what the passage means.

Check your answers on page 162

Passage 5

FINANCE CHARGE: The monthly finance charge is computed as follows:

- 2% of the average daily balance (up to $300)
- 1% of the part of the average daily balance over $300

PAYMENTS: You must pay at least the following amounts by the 27th day of each month:

- 10% of the average daily balance (up to $500)
- 20% of the part of the average daily balance over $500

1. On what type of form would you expect to find the above passage?

(a) a book or record club form
(b) an income tax form
(c) an application for automobile insurance
(d) an application for a credit card

2. If your unpaid balance were $100, how would the finance charge for that month be computed?
(a) 1% of $100
(b) 2% of $100
(c) 2% of $300
(d) 10% of $100

3. If your unpaid balance were $400, how would the finance charge for that month be computed?
(a) 2% of $300
(b) 2% of $400
(c) 2% of $300 plus 1% of $100
(d) 10% of $300 plus 20% of $100

4. If your average daily balance for the month were $300, how would the minimum payment for that month be computed?
(a) 2% of $300
(b) 10% of $300
(c) 10% of $500
(d) 20% of $300

5. If your average daily balance for the month were $1,000, how would the minimum payment for that month be computed?
(a) 2% of $300 plus 1% of $700
(b) 10% of $1,000
(c) 10% of $500 plus 20% of $500
(d) 20% of $1,000

Check your answers on page 163

Watch Part 3

In this lesson, you have become familiar with some of the things you will find on forms. You have seen what information is asked on almost every form and how you are to fill in this information. You also have seen what kinds of sentences and passages frequently appear on forms.

Vocabulary Review

The following vocabulary exercise is based on the vocabulary words at the beginning of this lesson. For each sentence, choose the correct word from the list below and write that word in the space provided. (Each word is used only once.)

anemic	consent	outstanding
ally	creditor	party affiliation
applicant	finance charge	platform
authorize	flier	polls
cast my ballot	invalid	primary
comprehensive insurance	liability insurance	register

1. Every month she has to pay a 1.5% __________ on her credit card balance.

2. If you do not vote at least once in two years, you will have to __________ again.

3. A person who suffers from an inadequate amount of red blood cells is said to be __________.

4. The man on the corner handed Isabelle a __________ that listed reduced rates for carpet cleaning.

5. In some cases, if you miss a loan payment, the __________ has the right to demand that you pay the entire unpaid balance at once.

6. The winner of the Democratic __________ will have to face the Republican candidate in November.

7. Is he our __________, or will he be working for our competitors?

8. The bank wants to know if I will __________ to let them investigate my credit records.

9. The warranty for most products becomes __________ if you abuse or mishandle the product.

10. I was asked to sign a form saying that I __________ the doctor to perform whatever surgery he thinks is necessary.

11. The insurance salesman told Margie that if she wants her car to be covered in case of theft, she must get __________.

12. Have you paid all of the bills yet, or are there still some __________?

13. The candidate said that it is important for every registered voter to go to the __________ on election day.

14. The __________ for the job sat in a room and waited to be called in for an interview.

15. What is your __________—Democrat, Republican, or Independent?

16. After listening to the political party's __________, I realized that I agreed with all of their positions on the issues.

17. In some states, all car owners must have __________ insurance, which is insurance that covers injuries to others and damage to property.

18. When election day comes, I will __________ for the candidate I think will do the most for our community.

Check your answers on page 163

Reading Skills Review

Exercise 2

In order to vote in a federal, state, or local election, you first must register with the local board of elections. To register to vote, you must fill out an application like the one on the next two pages:

Side 1:

APPLICATION FOR REGISTRATION AND ENROLLMENT BY MAIL

INSTRUCTIONS FOR APPLICANTS

(Read Instructions Carefully Before Filling Out Form)

1. **Application must be signed in two places—once on front and once on back, opposite arrow.**

2. The applicant must be a citizen of the United States and will be 18 years old and a resident of the county, city, or village for 30 days by election day.

3. If your county of residence is different from pre-printed address on reverse side, cross out address and substitute with appropriate address from above listing.

4. The completed application must be **received** by the county board of elections not later than the 30th day before the next following general or special election in order to qualify the applicant to vote in such election.

5. Applicants who have previously registered do not need to reregister unless they have moved or failed to vote in at least one election during the two preceding calendar years.

6. An applicant has the right to appear personally at his county board of elections to register during the period of central registration.

7. Enrollment in a political party is optional but if the applicant wishes to vote in a primary election of a political party he must be enrolled in that party. Failure to check one of the boxes in the Enrollment section of the application shall be construed as a desire by the applicant to be unaffiliated.

8. The application of a new registrant who enrolls in a political party must be received by the county board of elections not later than the 60th day before a primary election in order to qualify the applicant to vote in such election except that a person who did not possess the qualifications to vote at the preceding general election may submit his application up to 31 days before a primary election.

9. A person who is registered and who moves within the State of New York may transfer his registration and enrollment by completing this form. Applications must be received by the county board of elections not later than the 31st day before a primary election in order to qualify the applicant to vote in such election.

10. A person who is already registered from his present address may change his party enrollment by completing this form. Such change must be made not later than the 31st day preceding a general election in order to qualify the applicant to vote in the next following primary election (a change between non-affiliation and party affiliation is considered a change of enrollment).

11. If additional assistance or information should be required, please telephone one of the boards of election listed above.

ABSENTEE VOTING

In order for a person to be eligible to receive an absentee ballot for a general, special or primary election he must be on the day of such election sick or physically disabled or away from the county of his residence because of business or vacation.

If you desire an absentee ballot application from, please check the box below.

Primary ☐ General ☐

This is not an application for an absentee ballot.

If you wish application sent to an address other than below please note address.

____

____

____

It is a Class E felony for any applicant to procure a false registration or to furnish false information to the boards of election.

FOLD UP ON PERFORATION FIRST THIS WILL BE YOUR PERMANENT RECORD—PLEASE PRINT OR TYPE CLEARLY IN BLUE OR BLACK INK

0 (1) Last Name | First Name | Initial | Jr. or Sr. | Name and Address or Employer

RESIDENCE ADDRESS

1 (2) No | Street or Road | City or town, zip code | Mailing address if different | Village

2 (3) Date of birth | Sex | Height | Color of eyes | Telephone No (if listed) | If Apartment Dweller: Rm No, Floor No, Apt No | Length of time at residence: Years, Mos, Days

3 (4) **Did you previously vote in New York State? Yes ☐ No ☐ If yes, complete following line.**

In what year did you last vote in an election in this State? | Did you register under your present name? Yes ☐ No ☐ | If not, under what name did you register? | Did you then reside at you present address ____ If no, previous address— Street ____ City or town ____ County ____

(5) **Born in U.S.A.? Yes ☐ No ☐ If no, complete following line.**

Naturalization papers Own ☐ Mother ☐ Spouse ☐ Father ☐ | Number on papers | Date of papers | Court | City and State | Name of person to whom issued

(6) **ENROLLMENT**

(check only ONE)

If you wish to enroll in a political party, check the party of your choice:

☐ Democratic ☐ Republican

☐ Conservative ☐ Right to Life ☐ Liberal

☐ I do not wish to enroll in any political party.

☐ Transfer my present party enrollment to my new address (See instruction No. 9)

☐ I am herewith changing my enrollment (See instruction No. 10)

(7) **AFFIDAVIT**

"I affirm that the information provided herein is true and I understand that this application will be accepted for all purposes as the equivalent of an affidavit, and if it contains a material false statement, shall subject me to the same penalties for perjury as if I had been duly sworn."

Signature or Mark of Applicant Date

Witness to Mark (only if applicant is unable to sign) Date

FOR OFFICIAL USE ONLY

Election District | A.D (or Ward)

Date of reg.

Cancellation

Date ____

Reason 1 ☐ 2 ☐ 3 ☐ 4 ☐ 5 ☐ 6 ☐ 7 ☐ 8 ☐ 9 ☐ 10 ☐

Other Remarks

Democratic Register

Republican Register

ALSO SIGN ON REVERSE SIDE

FOR OFFICIAL USE ONLY

Serial No. | Last Name | First Name | Initial | Jr. or Sr. | Street address | City or town | E D | Wd or AD

Side 2:

3 2 1 0

APPLICANT

Sign your name in box opposite arrow. Make no other entry on this side.

YEAR	MONTH	IF PAPER BALLOTS ARE USED — NO. ON BALLOT — DELIVERED	VOTED	IF TWO MACHINES ARE USED — MACHINE DESIGNATION	MACHINE PUBLIC COUNTER NUMBER	SIGNATURE OF VOTER	INSPECTORS INITIALS
22							
21							
20							
19							
18							
17							
16							
15							
14							
13							
12							
11							
10							
9							
8							
7							
6							
5							
4							
3							
2							
1							

REGISTRATION SIGNATURE ⟹ X

CHALLENGED DATE														
ASSISTED DATE														

ENROLLMENT AND CHANGE OF ENROLLMENT

ENROLLMENT NUMBER	DATE	PARTY	REMARKS	INITIALS OF BOARD MEMBERS

1. According to section 5 of the instructions, under what conditions must a person who has previously registered fill out this form?

2. In order to vote in a general election, when must the county board of elections receive the completed application?

3. Under what conditions can a person get an absentee ballot?

4. Your name is Marion C. Diamond. Fill in this information in the appropriate section of the form.

5. You have never before been a registered voter in this state. How would you fill out section 4 of the form?

6. You are 5 feet, 4 inches tall. Fill in this information in the appropriate section of the form.

7. You would like to vote in the upcoming Democratic primary. How would you fill in section 6 of the form?

8. Your name is Marion C. Diamond. How would you fill in side 2 of the form?

Check your answers on page 164

Exercise 3

Before a doctor will operate on you, you often must fill out a hospital consent form. Look over the hospital consent form on the next page. Then answer the questions that follow. Parts of the form are numbered to make it easier to refer to these parts in the questions.

COUNTY GENERAL HOSPITAL

AUTHORIZATION FOR MEDICAL AND/OR SURGICAL TREATMENT

I, the undersigned, a patient of County General Hospital, hereby authorize such treatment as is necessary. I also authorize Dr. **1** ______________________________

and whomever he may designate as his assistants, to perform the following operation or procedure:

2 ______________________________

and such additional procedures as are considered therapeutically necessary or expedient on the basis of findings during the course of the operation and/or procedure. I also consent to the administration of such anesthetics as are necessary. Any tissues or parts surgically removed may be disposed of by the hospital in accordance with accustomed practice.

I hereby certify that I have read and fully understand the above authorization for medical and/or surgical procedure. The reasons the procedure or surgery is considered necessary were explained to me by Dr. **3** ______________________________. I also certify that no guarantee or assurance has been made as to the results that may be obtained.

4 ______________________________ (WITNESS)

5 ______________________________ (SIGNATURE OF PATIENT)

DATE: **6** ______________________________

TIME: **7** ______________________________

IF PATIENT IS UNABLE TO CONSENT OR IS A MINOR, COMPLETE THE FOLLOWING:

Patient is a minor **8** ________ years of age, or is unable to consent because: **9** ______________________________

____

____

10 ______________________________ (WITNESS)

11 ______________________________ (CLOSEST RELATIVE OR LEGAL GUARDIAN)

DATE: **12** ______________________________

TIME: **13** ______________________________

1. Your name is Herman Sawyer. Fill in this information in the appropriate section of the form.

2. The name of your doctor is Doctor Paul Lederman. Fill in this information in the appropriate section of the form.

3. You are having a tonsillectomy done. On what line of the form would you fill in this information?
   (a) line 1
   (b) line 2
   (c) line 3
   (d) line 5

4. The doctor who explained why you need this surgery is Dr. Lederman. On what line of the form would you fill in this information?
   (a) line 1
   (b) line 2
   (c) line 3
   (d) line 4

5. In your own words, state the meaning of the line, "I also certify that no guarantee or assurance has been made as to the results that may be obtained."

6. Based on the information in the form, you can conclude that if you fill out the form,
   (a) the doctor must awaken you and ask your permission if another operation is necessary
   (b) the doctor definitely will perform more than one operation
   (c) the doctor can use whatever anesthetics he feels are necessary
   (d) the doctor guarantees that the operation will be a success

Check your answers on page 165

Exercise 4

Before a bank or finance company will agree to give you a loan, you must show them you will be able to repay the loan. Thus, on a loan application, you must provide information about your job, your income, and how much you already owe. Look over the loan application on the next two pages. Then answer the questions that follow.

Side 1

READ TO LOAN APPLICANT(S): If married, you have the right to apply for separate individual credit in your own name. DATE

1 Individual Credit ☐ Joint Credit ☐ Co-Maker ☐ | Amount Requested: $ | Reason: | Source: P M O | Social Security #

APPLICANT NO. 1

If this is and application for Joint Credit, applicants choose who is Applicant No. 1 for mailing and record keeping purposes.

2 Last Name | First Name | Middle Initial | Other Names Used for Credit

3 Street and Mail Addresses (if different) 1. 2. | City | State | Zip

4 Birth Year | # of Dependents | Phone# [Y] Home [N] Nearby | ☐ I own ☐ I rent ☐ furnished ☐ unfurnished ☐ Other | Rent per Month $

5 Name (Landlord-Mortgages) | Address | Since Mo./Yr.

6 Previous Address (If at present address less than 3 years) 1. 2. | Previous Landlords & Addresses | How long

7 Employer's Name | Employed Since Mo./Yr.

8 Employer's Address | Work Phone & Ext.

9 Previous Employer (If at present job less than 3 years) 1. 2. | Address | How long

10 Occupation | Pay Day | Dept. or Badge # | Auto Makes 1. 2. | Yr. | Model

11 Bank or Credit Union Account ☐ Checking ☐ Self ☐ w/Another ☐ Savings ☐ Self ☐ w/Another | Bank and Branch | Auto Insurance: Type ______ Company ______ | Expires Mo./Yr.

Residence Purchase Price $ ______
Present Value $ ______
1st Mortgage $ ______
2nd Mortgage $ ______
Monthly Mortgage Including taxes $ ______ | Total Mortgage $ ______ Present Equity $ ______
Home Insurance Type:
Coverage Amount $ ______
Company:
My take home pay (excluding overtime) $ ______ monthly

IMPORTANT
READ TO APPLICANT THIS NOTICE
You need not disclose alimony, child support or separate maintenance income if you do not wish to have it considered as a basis for repaying this obligation.
I have other income from:
______ $ ______
source
TOTAL INCOME $ ______ monthly

12 FOR INDIVIDUAL SECURED CREDIT ONLY-AND ALL INDIVIDUAL LOANS IN COMMUNITY PROPERTY STATES
Applicant's marital status: ☐ Married ☐ Unmarried (Includes single, ☐ Separated divorced or widowed)
State name and address of each person other than applicant with an ownership interest in the security:

APPLICANT NO. 2

Enter a "dash" or "same" if information duplicates facts given by Applicant No. 1.

Social Security #

13 Last Name | First Name | Middle Initial | Other Names Used for Credit

14 Street and Mail Address (if different) 1. 2. | City | State | Zip

15 Birth Year | # of Dependents | Phone # [Y] Home [N] Nearby | ☐ I own ☐ I rent ☐ furnished ☐ unfurnished ☐ Other | Rent per Month $

16 Name (Landlord-Mortgages) | Address | Since Mo./Yr.

17 Previous Address (if at present address less than 3 years) 1. 2. | Previous Landlords & Addresses | How long

18 Employer's Name | Employed Since Mo./Yr.

19 Employer's Address | Work Phone & Ext.

20 Previous Employer (if at present job less than 3 years) 1. 2. | Address | How long

21 Occupation 1. 2. | Pay Day | Dept. or Badge # | Auto Makes 1. 2. | Yr. | Model

22 Bank or Credit Union Account ☐ Checking ☐ Self ☐ W/Another ☐ Savings ☐ Self ☐ W/Another | Bank and Branch | Auto Insurance. Type ______ Company ______ | Expires Mo./Yr.

Residence Purchase Price $ ______
Present Value $ ______
1st Mortgage $ ______
2nd Mortgage $ ______
Monthly Mortgage Including taxes $ ______ | Total Mortgage $ ______ Present Equity $ ______
Home Insurance Type:
Coverage Amount $ ______
Company:
My take home pay (excluding overtime) $ ______ monthly

IMPORTANT
READ TO APPLICANT THIS NOTICE
You need not disclose alimony, child support or separate maintenance income if you do not wish to have it considered as a basis for repaying this obligation.
I have other income from:
______ $ ______
TOTAL INCOME $ ______
TOTAL BOTH APPS $ ______

23 FOR JOINT CREDIT (Secured or Unsecured)
Marital Status: Applicant No. 1: Married ☐ Separated ☐ Unmarried ☐ Applicant No. 2: Married ☐ Separated ☐ Unmarried ☐ (Includes single, divorced or widowed) | Relationship of applicants, if any:

24

Military Applicants Only		Serial #	Date Enlistment Expires	Name and Phone of C.O.
	Applicant No. 1			
	Applicant No. 2			

Side 2

ALL APPLICANTS LIST ALL DEBTS-ATTACH A SEPARATE SHEET IF NECESSARY TO COMPLETE THE LIST

		CREDITOR AND LOCATION	ACCOUNT NUMBER	MONTHLY PAYMENT	PRESENT BALANCE	Check Status Current	Check Status Past Due
25	BANK, CREDIT UNION AND FINANCE COMPANY LOANS.						
26							
27							
28							
29							
30							
31	STORE ACCTS.						
32							
33	DEPARTMENT CHARGE						
34							
35							
36	MAJOR CREDIT CARD						
37							
38							
39	OTHER						
40							

41 TOTAL $______

	APP [1]	CAP	APP [2]
1			
2			
3			
4			
5			
6			
7			
8			
9			
10			
Sub Total			
11			
12			
[J] Total			
Capped By		Capped By	
Checked By		Checked By	

This list of all my debts accurately reflects the information given to you by me personally or by telephone. I have read this listing and I affirm that this is a complete listing of all my debts.

42 Signature - Applicant No. 1 ______ Date ______ Witness Signature ______ Date ______

43 Signature - Applicant No. 2 ______ Date ______ Witness Signature ______ Date ______

44

OFFICE USE ONLY

SECURITY RATIO

HHG $ ______
AUTO $ ______
LOAN VALUE OF REAL ESTATE $ ______
OTHER $ ______
TOTAL SECURITY $ ______
NET AMT. OF LOAN $ ______
RATIO (TOTAL/LOAN) ______ %

ABILITY EVALUATION

FIXED EXPENSES PER MO. — TOTAL INCOME PER MO.

$ ______ TOTAL CURRENT MONTHLY PAYMENTS
$ ______ NEW LOAN PAYMENT
$ ______ HOUSING COSTS
$ ______ TOTAL FIXED EXPENSE $ ______

BALANCE FOR ALL OTHER LIVING COSTS $ ______ Per MO.

DEBT RATIO

$ ______ Total Income
$ ______ Total Fixed Expenses

BENCOM LOAN INPUTS - DO NOT USE FOR ISC

45 Monthly Pay Amt. (4) | No Payments (x5) | Amt. Note Total Repayable (6) | DUE DAY (7) | SECUR Code (8) | SOURCE Code (9) | FILING FEES Rec. or Ref. (10) | Lic, Title+/or Reg (11) | REASON Code (12) | ACCOUNT NO. (PB, FB, RE) (13) | CPO Code (14) | CBI Code (15) | STD Code (16)

46 LIFE & DISABILITY Type Code (17A) | PROPERTY: Type Code (17B) | Term Code (17C) | HHC Term (Mos.) (18A) | Dwelling Term (Mos.) (18B) | Rate Code (18C) | LEAVE BLANK (18D) | HHC PREMIUM (19A) | DWELLING PREMIUM (19B)

47 INSURANCE CODES

17A
1-Decreasing Term on Borrower
2-Decreasing Term on Borrower & Spouse
3-Level Term on Borrower
4-Level Term on Borrower & Spouse
6-Disability and Decreasing Term on Borrower
7-Disability on Borrower Decreasing Term on Borrower & Spouse
8-Disability and Level Term on Borrower
9-Disability on Borrower Level Term on Borrower & Spouse

17B
1-Household Contents
2-Dwelling
3-HHContents & Dwelling
4-Homeowners

17C
0-HHC and/or Dwelling Term-Less than 100 Months
1-HHC Term-100 Months or more
2-Dwelling Term-100 Months or more
3-Both Terms-100 Months or more

18C
10-HHContents
01-Dwelling
11-HHC and Dwelling

48 TRAN CODE | TAB | TAB | TAB | SOC SEC NO | ADDR | YB | D | M | T | FBLN | P/O | CAP VALUE | CREDIT LIMIT | S OL | H | APPLICANT #1 DT EMP | OCC | Q DT. EMP. | APPLICANT #2 R INCOME | S OCC | T TOTAL INCOME

1. Your name is Elizabeth Mary Gregory. You want all information about the loan to be mailed to you. Fill in your name on the appropriate line of the form.

2. On what line of the form would you put the name of the person who is applying for the loan with you?

3. You are asking for a $2,500 loan in order to buy a used car. Fill in this information in the appropriate section of the form.

4. You work for the Union Grocers on 17 Main Street, Union City, Alabama 61534. You have worked there since August 5, 1979. Your telephone number at work is area code 613, 532-1764. Fill in this information in the appropriate section of the form.

5. Your home is presently worth $45,000. Fill in this information on the appropriate line of the form.

6. The person who is applying for the loan with you takes home $725 per month. Fill in this information on the appropriate line of the form.

7. You have a charge account at Franklin's Department Store in Union City, Ala. Your account number is 6314725. Your average payment is $35 per month. Your current balance is $375. Fill in this information in the appropriate section of the form.

8. You have a liability insurance policy for your car with the Home Mutual Insurance Company. This insurance policy expires in December of 1984. Fill in this information in the appropriate section of the form.

9. On which of the following lines should you not write anything?
   (a) line 6
   (b) line 16
   (c) line 42
   (d) line 45

Check your answers on page 165

Exercise 5

By taking out a life insurance policy, you make sure that when you die, your family will have enough money to survive. There are basically two types of life insurance:

- *Term life insurance* covers you for a limited period of time. Under the term life plan, the money you have paid in premiums is kept by the insurance company when the policy expires.
- *Whole life insurance* covers you for life. Under the whole life plan, the money you have paid in premiums is returned to you if the policy expires.

Look over the life insurance application on the next two pages. Then answer the questions that follow.

Side 1

PART A

NO. 109

Application To **FIRST CITY LIFE INSURANCE COMPANY**

Questions 1-9, 19-28 and 36-39 Refer To Proposed Insured

Policy Number

Agency Name and Number

1. Full Name of Proposed Insured (Print First, Middle and Last Name)

2. Social Security No.

3. Birthdate (Mo.-Day-Yr.)

4. Sex ☐ M ☐ F

5. Birthplace

6. Issue Policy At Age

7. Residence Address (Give Street and Number, City or Town, State and Zip Code)

8. A. Employer and Kind of Business

B. Business Address

9. A. Occupation

B. How Long in Present Occupation?

C. Any Change Contemplated? Yes ☐ No ☐ (If "Yes" Explain in Remarks)

IF LIFE INSURANCE IS APPLIED FOR, ANSWER QUESTIONS 1-9 AND 10-28

10. Plan

11. Amount

12. Additional Benefits

☐ Waiver of Premiums
☐ Accidental Death Benefit $
☐ YRT Rider $
☐ ____ Yr. Reducing Term Rider ____% $
☐ Additional Insurance Option $
☐ Children Protection Benefit (Complete Form 1455)
☐ Family Protection Benefit (Complete Form 1440)
☐ ______ Units of Cost of Living Rider

14A. Premium Interval

☐ Annual - 12 Months
☐ Semi Annual - 6 Months
☐ Quarterly - 3 Months
☐ Monthly - 1 Month
☐ COM - 1 Month

14B. Special Billing Type

☐ Group
☐ Payroll Deduction
☐ Gov. Allotment

15. Use of Dividend

☐ Cash
☐ Applied (N/A COM)
☐ Dividends Held
☐ Dividend Additions
☐ Deferred Additions
☐ Dividend Term Option
Balance To ________

16. Send Premium Notice To:

☐ Residence Address #7
☐ Business Address #8
☐ Owner's Address #13
☐ Other (Give Name & Address)

13. Owner: (If Owner is a Minor Complete Form 1481)

☐ Insured
☐ ______________________________, A
______________________ Corporation, its Successors or Assigns
☐ ______________________________ While Living,
Thereafter ______________________________
Contingent Owner While Living, and Thereafter
Check One { ☐ The Executors or Administrators of Last Survivor of The Named Owners
☐ Insured }
☐ As Per Supplemental Request

Owner's Address ______________________________

Owner's Soc. Sec. or Taxpayer Ident. No.

17. Automatic Payment of Premium is Requested.

18. Beneficiary: (Give full names, dates of birth and relationships to Proposed Insured)

First

Second

Payment will be shared equally by all first beneficiaries who survive insured; if none, by all second beneficiaries who so survive; if none, payment will be made to owner or executors or administrators of the owner's estate.

☐ As per supplemental request

The right to change the beneficiary is reserved.

19. Do you now smoke cigarettes or have you smoked any cigarettes within the last 12 months? Yes ☐ No ☐

20. Life Insurance in force (If "None", so state)

Company (Including Group)	Total Amount	Total With Waiver of Premiums	Total Accidental Death Benefit
	$	$	$

21. A. Has there been or will there be a lapse, surrender, reissue, or conversion (to reduce amount, premium or period of coverage) of any existing life, disability or annuity contract if the applied for policy is issued? Yes ☐ No ☐

B. Will there be any substantial borrowing on any life insurance policy if the applied for policy is issued? Yes ☐ No ☐

(If either or both questions are answered "Yes" give in remarks complete name of company and policy number. If disability insurance is being replaced give termination date also)

22. Have you ever applied for life, health or disability insurance or reinstatement of life, health or disability insurance which was declined, postponed or modified in any way? (If "Yes" give details in remarks) Yes ☐ No ☐

23. Have you ever been or do you have any intention of becoming a pilot or crew member of any type of aircraft? (If "Yes" complete aviation form 1487) Yes ☐ No ☐

24. Have you within the last two years participated in or do you intend to participate in, any motor powered racing, scuba, skin or sky diving, rodeos or any other avocation generally considered hazardous? (If "Yes" complete avocation form 1390) Yes ☐ No ☐

25. Do you intend to travel or reside outside the U.S.A.? (If "Yes" complete foreign travel form 1480) Yes ☐ No ☐

26. Are you or do you have any intention of becoming a member of a military organization? (If "Yes" give company, amount & reason in remarks) Yes ☐ No ☐

27. Are other negotiations for life or disability insurance pending? (If "Yes" give company, amount & reason in remarks) Yes ☐ No ☐

28. Have you had your motor vehicle driving license suspended or revoked during the last two years? (If "Yes" give details in remarks) Yes ☐ No ☐

Side 2

IF DISABILITY INSURANCE IS APPLIED FOR, ANSWER QUESTIONS 1-9 AND 20-39

29. Plan and Amount ☐ SAO ☐ SAO Step Rate ☐ SA1 ☐ SA2

	Basic Policy	ADI Rider	ADI Rider
Monthly Income:	$ ______	$ ______	$ ______
Commencement Date:			
Accident Benefit Period:	______	______	______
Sickness Benefit Period:	______	______	______

☐ SA3 ☐ SA4 } Complete form SA101 — Maximum Monthly Overhead Expense Benefit: $ ______

30. Additional Benefits

☐ Residual Disability Income

☐ Hospital Benefit: $ ______ Per Month

☐ Lifetime Sickness: $ ______ Per Month

☐ Additional Insurance Option: $ ______ Per Month

☐ Accidental Death and Dismemberment: $ ______

Beneficiary:

Relationship:

31. Use of Dividends: ☐ Cash ☐ Applied (N/A COM)

32. Owner

Owner's Address ______

Owner's Soc. Sec. or Taxpayor Ident No. ______

33A. Premium Interval

☐ Annual—12 Months ☐ Quarterly - 3 Months

☐ Semiannual—6 Months ☐ COM - 1 Month

33 B. Special Billing Type

☐ Group

☐ Payroll Deduction

34. Send Premium Notice To: ☐ Residence Address #7 ☐ Business Address #8 ☐ Owner's Address #32 ☐ Other (Give Name & Address)

35. Is the employer paying the premium? ☐ Yes ☐ No

36. Annual Earned Income: from employer: $ ______

Other sources: $ ______ (Give sources in remarks)

37. Is any of your income guaranteed during disability as part of a formal salary continuation or sick leave plan? Yes ☐ No ☐

If "yes" ______% or $ ______ for ______ months

38. Do you understand and agree that for each separate period of disability no total disability benefit is payable until the commencement date specified in section 29? Yes ☐ No ☐

39. Disability insurance in force (If "None", so state)

Company (Including Group)	Monthly Benefit	Benefit Period	Purpose Personal Income Bus. Overhead Expn Buy/Sell	Company (Including Group)	Monthly Benefit	Benefit Period	Purpose: Personal Income Bus. Overhead Expn. Buy/Sell

40. Home office corrections and amendments:

41. Remarks and additional directions:

(1) The statements and answers on Part A of this application are to the best knowledge and belief of the proposed insured, complete and true. They together with the statements and answers on part B of this application shall be a part of the contract of insurance if one be issued. The applicant, if someone other than the proposed insured agrees to be bound by all statements and answers signed by the proposed insured in parts A and B of this application. (2) The agent taking this application has no authority to make, change or discharge any contract hereby applied for. The agent may not extend credit on behalf of the Company. No statement made to or information acquired by any representative of the Company shall bind the Company unless set out in writing in parts A or B of this application. (3) The Company shall incur no liability under any policy issued on this application unless and until: (A) such policy is delivered to the owner; and (B) the first premium is paid during the continued insurability of the insured. Any conditional receipt issued, which bears the same number as this application, may provide otherwise. (4) Acceptance of any policy issued on this application will ratify any correction in or amendment to the application noted by the Company in the space headed "Home Office corrections or amendments." A copy of the amended application attached to the policy will be sufficient notice of the change made. If the laws where the application is made so require, any change of amount, class of risk, plan of insurance or benefits must be ratified in writing.

I have paid $ ______ for Life Insurance, $ ______ for Disability Insurance with this application. I have received a conditional receipt and have read it and understand it.

AUTHORIZATION

I, the proposed insured, hereby authorize any licensed physician, medical practitioner, hospital, clinic or other medical or medically related facility, insurance company, the Medical Information Bureau or other organization, institution or person, that has any records or knowledge of me or my health, to give to the First City Life Insurance Company or its Reinsurers any such information. I also acknowledge receipt or copies of the pre-notifications relating to investigative consumer reports and the Medical Information Bureau. A photographic copy of this authorization shall be as valid as the original.

Signed at ______ (PLACE) ______ (DATE) 19 ____

______ Applicant ______ Proposed insured

Sign name in full — Sign name in full

Only one signature required when proposed insured is the applicant

1. Your name is Susan Ann Galindez. Your Social Security number is 131-58-9229. You were born on September 5, 1939, in Brooklyn, New York. Your address is 179 9th Avenue, Brooklyn, NY 10229. Fill in this information in the appropriate sections of the form.

2. You have worked as a secretary at the Galaxy Shoe Manufacturers, 175 Cedarview Drive, Brooklyn, NY 10342, for 15 years. You have no intention of changing jobs. Fill in this information in the appropriate section of the form.

3. You would like to be insured for $50,000 under the whole life insurance plan. You would like to pay your premium once every three months. Fill in this information in the appropriate section of the form.

4. A beneficiary is the person who will get the insurance money when you die. You would like your husband, William Galindez, born on June 29, 1937, and your daughter, Stephanie Galindez, born on November 12, 1963, to share the insurance money equally. Fill in this information in the appropriate section of the form.

5. If you were applying only for life insurance and not for disability insurance, which of the following sections would you NOT fill out?
   (a) section 7
   (b) section 13
   (c) section 24
   (d) section 29

6. If you were applying only for disability insurance and not for life insurance, which of the following sections would you NOT fill out?
   (a) section 2
   (b) section 10
   (c) section 24
   (d) section 33A

7. In your own words, state what the first sentence in the *authorization* section of the form means.

Check your answers on page 166

TV Scripts— "More Pages"

ACT I
"The Contract That Binds"

Rhonda is shopping in the Big Twix Department Store, where she was allowed to open a charge account. Bobby is accompanying her; they are strolling down the aisle with a shopping cart.

RHONDA: ... so anyway, after I got the credit forms all taken care of, Ruby showed me a copy of another form that was a whole lot more interesting than those credit ones.

BOBBY: the only forms I know anything about are the daily racing forms!

RHONDA: Anyway, this form Ruby showed me—it was a marriage contract.

Bobby is a little startled by the word marriage; Rhonda notices his reaction.

RHONDA: Relax, will you. The last thing I need right now is another husband. One was about enough to do me in. All I need is a boyfriend. Boyfriends don't have the claims on you that husbands do. Or, that husbands *think* they do.

BOBBY: I don't even like to talk about it!

The camera tracks them from the front as they continue down the aisle.

RHONDA: Anyway, this marriage contract form that Ruby had was real interesting, because by signing it the husband and wife agree that if they ever split up, they'll divide whatever they have equally—fifty/fifty.

Bobby stops in his tracks.

BOBBY: What if the man has a big savings account before he gets married? What about that?

RHONDA: What if it's the woman who has a big savings account? Either way, there's a part in there about that. It says that they get back whatever they started with and then half of whatever they save while they're together.

Bobby shakes his head and half turns away as if he thinks it's too silly to talk about any more.

BOBBY: Even if the man makes it all? That don't sound right.

Rhonda's warming up.

RHONDA: Yup, that's right all right. 'Cause if he's making it all you can bet your bootie the woman's pulling her weight at home: taking care of the kids, cleaning the house, cooking, doing the laundry.

Rhonda recaptures Bobby's attention by throwing a box of disposable diapers at him; then she pushes a broom at him; then a pot from a nearby shelf; and then a box of laundry soap; he catches each kind of clumsily and angrily sticks them in the shopping cart.

RHONDA: And I'll bet you a lot of women are doing all that and working a job, too. Only, when they do a job they don't get paid the same as a man would for doing the same job! I read that in the paper. If they paid women the same as they pay men, then maybe women would bring home as much as men. Why, they'd probably bring home more, since men seem to lose a lot of their pay at the bar on the way home!

Bobby's getting mad now.

BOBBY: Who-eee! I never thought I'd have a date with a women's-liber-ater-type woman, no sir!

Rhonda pushes the cart off at full speed, without even looking back.

RHONDA: Yeah, I wonder if you'll ever have one again! I'll see if I can't find myself a liberated man....

She refuses to stop.

BOBBY: Hold on there; hey, come back here. What's she talking about now? A liberated man? What is that?

Bobby is left talking to himself.

Fade out on Bobby in the aisle alone.

ACT II
"Saving Grace"

Martin and Gloria are sitting in the living room on the couch, which doubles as Darrell's bed; Darrell comes into the room brushing his teeth.

DARRELL: I hate to ruin your party, but do you think you two could move off of my bed? I need my rest, you understand! What's that you're messing with, anyway?

Martin gives him an angry look.

GLORIA: We're filling out the census form, Darrell. We'll be done in a few minutes and then you can have your bed.

DARRELL: Census form? How come you're bothering with that? It's just more of the government bull.

MARTIN: I'll tell you why we're fooling with it. I saw Mean Joe Greene, the football player, on a TV commercial the other night. He said we ought to fill out the census form because the government uses the information they get from these things to help decide where to spend our tax money.

GLORIA: Yeah, and the more people around here that fill these out, the more local improvements we get in the neighborhood.

DARRELL: Maybe they can improve my sleeping conditions!

Martin pretends to ignore Darrell.

MARTIN: Look here, Gloria, it says to list all the people that live in this apartment and how they are related. I'm gonna put myself down and I'll list you as my wife, but then I don't know how to list Darrell—it doesn't say anything about parasites, leeches, and loafers on this form.

He gives Darrell the evil eye.

DARRELL: Hey, what's he saying?

GLORIA: Martin, don't get nasty now.

DARRELL: Sometimes I get the feeling your husband don't like your little brother.

GLORIA: Darrell, I think Martin loves you, only it'd be easier for him to love you if you had your own apartment. You've been living with us a long time, and in this little apartment it just gets old sometimes.

Darrell's feelings get hurt.

GLORIA: Someday Martin and I would like to have a place of our own.... Listen, why don't you open up a savings account and save a little money so you can be more independent, maybe even get your own apartment.

MARTIN: Yeah, that's a good idea. Maybe Gloria's right. A savings account might be just what you need. Look here, little brother, I don't mean to sound so rough about it, but dammit, someday you got to get out on your own.

Darrell is sulking by now.

DARRELL: I don't want to fool around with any bank. I want my money in my pocket.

GLORIA: It stays in there a long time, huh? You ought to check into a savings account, I tell you.

DARRELL: The only time I'm gonna need a bank account is after I make my million—then I'll get one of those secret Swiss bank accounts to hide all my money.

Darrell goes back to brushing his teeth and ambles out of the room. Martin and Gloria eye him as he leaves.

Disssolve to pan of bank lobby; camera finally settles on a long shot of a man talking to a customer across a desk. Zoom in to show Darrell is the customer; he's signing something.

BANKER: ... This is your passbook; I've already recorded your $50 deposit in here. You'll need to bring this with you every time you want to make a deposit or a withdrawal. Occasionally you should ask the teller to check on your interest, or the amount of money your money is making for you while it's in the savings account. We pay 5.5 percent interest these days. That means if you leave $100 in your savings account for a year it will earn $5.50 in interest.

DARRELL: That sounds great.

BANKER: One thing that might help you save is a budget.

DARRELL: A budget?

BANKER: It'll help you figure out where your money goes.

DARRELL: That's one thing I've *never* been able to figure out—money just seems to disappear.

BANKER: Well, with a budget, you list your income and your expenses. And you divide your expenses into necessary expenses like food and clothing and what you might call discretionary expenses—things you don't really need but would like to have. Things like entertainment expenses, money to go on dates or go to the movies.

DARRELL: Those sound pretty necessary to me!

BANKER: Well, you figure how much you have coming in and how much you're going to have to shell out and then you see what's left over. Then you should take some of what's left over and put it into savings. Or even make savings a priority, or one of your necessary items. You might decide to put $25 a month into savings. Pick out a figure and try to stick with it.

DARRELL: Uh-huh, uh-huh. I'm getting the idea.

Dissolve to Darrell entering the apartment; he finds Martin reading the paper.

DARRELL: All right, Mr. Martin, ready for some good news?

MARTIN: You got an apartment?

DARRELL: Nope.

MARTIN: Too bad.

Darrell's acting proud of himself.

DARRELL: But it might not be too long; I went down and opened a savings account after I got paid today. I made my first deposit—$50.

Martin puts down the paper.

MARTIN: Hey, man, that's great! Now your money's making money for you.

Darrell's mood changes a little.

DARRELL: Yeah, I guess so. I'm already having second thoughts. By putting all that money in the bank, I didn't leave myself with any "discretionary" funds, to use the banker's words.

MARTIN: You mean you don't have any dough to go out tonight, huh? Well look, Darrell, to show you there are no hard feelings, I'll lend you a couple of bucks to go to the movie.

Darrell's mood swings back to a joking one once again.

DARRELL: A couple of bucks? A movie? Man, I need more coin than that! I'm talking about nightclubs and restaurants and bars—you're gonna have to do better than a couple of bucks!

Darrell and Martin make threatening gestures at each other, but it's all in fun.

MARTIN: And you're gonna have to get out of here before I get out of this chair and rearrange your head a little!

Fade out on the two of them grappling with each other.

ACT III
"Inside-Out Improvement Plan"

Gloria comes into the apartment and finds Darrell on the couch, filling out an order form; he has $22.50 in bills and coins taped to a piece of cardboard.

GLORIA: Hey, look at all that cash! What's up, Darrell?

DARRELL: Hey, Gloria. I'm just filling out this order form. I'm ordering something to improve my form, you might say. I'm sending for the Inside-Out Image Improvement Plan.

Gloria's tone is sarcastic.

GLORIA: What? You need *improving*??

Darrell points to a few bumps on his face.

DARRELL: Just some little problems that I need to eliminate. See these zits? They make me feel like a teenager again. Plus, I want to grow my hair out again and I want it to look good. Last time I did I couldn't get it to look right. I want it to look like the hair on this dude in the picture.

He hands her a magazine, opened to an advertisement for the I-O-I-I-Plan; the ad features a beautiful black man and a gorgeous black woman; their skin seems to glow and their hairdos are perfect Afros.

GLORIA: Yeah, they look pretty good, but ...

Darrell mocks her.

DARRELL: "But Darrell, but Darrell ..."—that's all you know how to say. Listen to this: "The Inside-Out Image Improvement Plan does not involve greasy creams or ointments that you apply on the outside. Scientifically formulated tablets work from within to correct deficiencies you may have that cause problems with skin and hair."

Darrell has a little trouble with the word "deficiencies."

DARRELL: You see, your body might have some kind of deficiency—you lack something you need in order to be healthy—and by taking these tablets, you can make up for it.

Gloria's getting a little angry.

GLORIA: Sounds familiar, if you ask me. Sounds like an ad for vitamins. "Do you have iron-deficiency anemia?" and all that business?

Darrell is, too.

DARRELL: You sound familiar, too! Always trying to bring down some idea I've got. It doesn't say anything on here about vitamins! Listen: "high-potency ingredients recommended by doctors, natural and safe, specially designed to attack your deficiencies from within."

GLORIA: Yeah, well, while those tablets are running around inside you maybe they can change your brain as well as your complexion! You've got money to spend on some kind of pills that are supposed to cure all your ills?

DARRELL: I know this isn't gonna cure every problem, but I've only got a couple of small deficiencies that are messing up my image.

GLORIA: Is your image that important? What's wrong with the way you look now? These models in this picture are *all image*. They don't look this good in real life. They just make 'em look like this for these magazine ads. It's just a trick. Besides, if you looked like this, you wouldn't be Darrell anymore. And I sort of like you the way you are. You understand what I'm saying?

DARRELL: What do you mean, they don't look this good in real life? Pictures don't lie!

GLORIA: Oh, yes, they can. But you're missing my point: You can't tell a book by its cover, you dig? It's not what's up front or what's outside that's important; it's what's inside you.

DARRELL: That's right, and that's why I'm gonna put those tablets inside me—so they can do their work in the right place.

Fade out.

Fade in on Darrell on the telephone; the words "Two weeks later" appear on the screen. As Darrell is finishing his conversation, Gloria enters from the other room.

DARRELL: ... Okay, thanks, yeah, I might just do that. But other than filling out the complaint form there's nothing much I can do, huh? ... Okay, sure. Thanks anyway.

He hangs up.

GLORIA: Complaint form? Who was that?

DARRELL: That was the Better Business Bureau.

Gloria notices a box on the table; she goes to it and picks a bottle out of it.

DARRELL: Remember that order form I filled out and mailed off a couple of weeks ago, for the Inside-Out Image Improvement Plan? The stuff came today; that's why I called the Better Business Bureau: to find out about filling out a complaint form. I hate to say it, but I been ripped off. You were right—I hate to say that, too—but those tablets are nothing but vitamins and minerals.

GLORIA: What about the money-back guarantee?

DARRELL: You have to use the tablets for a month before you can say you're not satisfied. It didn't say that on the order form! I got put in the old trick bag....

Gloria is still looking over the list of ingredients on the bottle.

GLORIA: Sometimes, that's what "image" is all about: tricking people into thinking you're something you're not.

DARRELL: That's right, go ahead and lay it on me. I deserve it.

GLORIA: But maybe you didn't get ripped off after all.

DARRELL: Huh?

GLORIA: Vitamins and minerals are good for you, you know. They might just make up for those deficiencies you were talking about.

DARRELL: Yeah?

GLORIA: As for your main deficiency, I'd have to recommend a transplant.

Darrell feels his head.

DARRELL: A hair transplant?

GLORIA: No, little brother, a *brain* transplant! I'll go get the knife!

DARRELL: Gloria?! Dawg, man, I wish you'd get a mouth transplant.

Fade out as they get into a playful game of the "druthers."

GLORIA: Oh, yeah, well I tell you what else you need ...

ACT IV
"Making Dates, the Modern Way"

Ronald is sitting in a tavern with his buddy, Barlow; they're sitting at the bar sipping on beers.

RONALD: Barlow, you know that song by the Statler Brothers—

Ronald sings a few lines from the song.

RONALD: "Counting Flowers on the Wall"? It's been going through my head for days, over and over. "I'm having lots of fun/ counting flowers on the wall/ don't bother me at all/ playing solitaire 'til dawn/ with a deck of 51/ watching Captain Kangaroo/ don't tell me I've nuthin' to do." Besides counting them, I'm becoming one.

BARLOW: One what?

RONALD: A wallflower, that's what. Now I know what old maids feel like. I'm not getting any younger, you know.

BARLOW: This reminds me of that song by Linda Ronstadt: "Poor, poor, pitiful me." You're getting into that old Hank Williams I'm-so-lonesome-I-could-die rut. You gotta snap out of it. Life's not always like they make it out to be in those country and western songs.

RONALD: But I don't know what to do! How do you meet girls in this city? If you just up and say "good evening" to them on the street, they act like you're a cottonmouth moccasin.

BARLOW: A lot of women don't like the real direct approach.

RONALD: So what do you do? You've had some dates lately; how'd you meet those girls?

BARLOW: Well, I thought I might hear more of your poor-mouthing tonight, so I came prepared.... I have here a ticket out of your lonely room.

Barlow reaches for something in his coat pocket.

RONALD: What's that thing?

BARLOW: This is a form you fill out when you join Singles Society. It's a club; you fill out this form and pay $25. They put your information into a computer that lines you up with girls you'll hit it off with.

Ronald is disappointed.

RONALD: Aw, I've heard about that kind of stuff before. It's too wild for me, man.

BARLOW: No, you've got the wrong idea. This isn't one of those bizarro-freako operations. You meet some real nice women. Really. That's how I got those dates I've had lately.

Ronald's interested again.

RONALD: Yeah? Well, how'd they go?

BARLOW: Great! Would I be telling you about it if it weren't a sure thing?

RONALD: So what do you put on that form, anyway?

BARLOW: Just some general information about yourself. Come on, I'll help you fill it out; you'll be out on the town this weekend with some fine-looking woman.

RONALD: All right, what do they want to know?

BARLOW: Oh, the regular stuff, like height, weight, and age. Then you answer a few simple questions so they can line you up with the right kind of women. Questions like: "What are your hobbies?" and "What are your favorite activities?" And it asks you to describe your best qualities. "What do you look for in someone of the opposite sex"—that's another one. And "What was the last book you read?" Simple questions like that.

Ronald puts his head in his hands; he's a little disgusted.

RONALD: Simple questions like that, huh? I can't answer those questions, Barlow! I don't know what to say. There's not much *to* say!

BARLOW: Then you make something up. It's just a form. Come on, let's start with your best qualities ...

Ronald stares straight ahead.

BARLOW: Drawing a blank, huh? How 'bout if we say you're easygoing ... good-looking ... smart ... and we'll throw in "shy"—some girls like that.

Barlow starts filling in the form.

RONALD: Sure, sure, put all that down. It doesn't matter, anyway.

BARLOW: Okay, what about your hobbies and favorite activities?

RONALD: Drinking beer and watching football on TV.

BARLOW: I'll spruce that up a little. "Enjoys cultural activities"—that's a good one to use.

Ronald gets more disgusted.

RONALD: Come off it, Barlow! Why don't you just say I'm divorced and lonely as hell and don't know what in the world to do with myself—tell it like it is.

BARLOW: Yeah, they'll come running when they hear that. Look, let's forget it. 'Scuse me for trying. Let's talk about football or something.

RONALD: I'm sorry, Barlow. It's just that questions like that—what are your best qualities—are hard for me to answer. I don't know if I have any!

BARLOW: Mmmm, that *is* low. But I wasn't out to rub salt in your wounds, you understand. I was just trying to help.

After a brief silence, Ronald speaks.

RONALD: Okay, go ahead and fill that thing out any way you want. I'll give you the $25 and we'll see what happens.

BARLOW: There you go!

RONALD: Tell me more about those dates you had. What were the girls like? What did you do?

BARLOW: Well, I've had four dates and they were all real nice girls. They had a good sense of humor.

RONALD: What do you mean?

BARLOW: I could have had more dates, but the others backed out. See, you're supposed to send a picture of yourself in with the form and they show it to the girls they think would like a date with you. I didn't have any photos of myself, so I clipped out one of Burt Reynolds from a magazine and sent it in. The girls that backed out didn't think it was funny, I guess. But the ones that did go were a lot of fun.

RONALD: Barlow, you're too much. So whose picture should I send in?

BARLOW: How 'bout that baseball pitcher who models in all those underwear ads?

Begin fade out.

RONALD: Yeah, that ought to do it. Now come on and tell me more about those dates. Did you kiss 'em good night? What did you talk about? Where did you go?

Fade completed.

Answers and Explanations

1st Intermission

1. Darrell has to fill out a voter registration form.
2. (b) Charles Coots tells Darrell you don't have to re-register as long as you vote at least once every two years.
3. Martin tells Darrell he can choose Democratic, Republican, or Independent.
4. Martin tells Darrell that if he wants to vote for Charles Coots in the primary, he will have to register for Charles Coots's party.
5. (c) Martin tells Darrell to take the completed form to the courthouse.
6. Rhonda thinks it is unfair because it was up to her to make sure all of the bills were paid.
7. (d) Candy tells Rhonda she found out about Ruby Hatton from the Women's Help Line.
8. Candy tells Rhonda that Ruby Hatton helps women for free because she wants to see women get a fair deal.

Exercise 1

1. You should keep in mind the following four tips:
   - Read all of the instructions that come with the form.
   - Use a pen or typewriter to fill out the form.
   - Print all information.
   - Do not leave anything blank unless it does not apply to you.
2.

NAME: ARMSTRONG (Last) JOSEPH (First) L (M.I.)

3.

DATE OF BIRTH: 2 / 9 / 54

4.

SOCIAL SECURITY NUMBER | 2 | 1 | 7 | - | 4 | 5 | - | 8 | 7 | 7 | 8 |

5.

ADDRESS: 135 Harvest Drive
Number and Street

Glendale WI 31425
City or Town State Zip

6.

TELEPHONE: (545) 323 - 4874

7.

MARITAL STATUS: Divorced

8.

DATE OF BIRTH | 1 | 0 | ■ | 2 | ■ | 4 | 0 |

9.

NAME: Edwards, John H.
Last First M.I.

10.

Marital Status	☑ Single	☐ Married	☐ Divorced
	☐ Separated	☐ Widowed	
Sex	(M) circled	F	

11.

HOME ADDRESS	NUMBER AND STREET: 3251 Richmond Avenue Apartment 12A			
	CITY: Rockland	STATE: CT.	ZIP: 17435	YEARS THERE: 12
PREVIOUS HOME ADDRESS (If less than 3 years at present address)	NUMBER AND STREET			
	CITY	STATE	ZIP	

12. A person whose husband has died is a widow.

Marital Status	☑ Single	☐ Married
(If separated, divorced, or widowed, check single.)		

13.

SOCIAL SECURITY NUMBER: 235 - 21 - 1245

14.

SIGNATURE: Marsha T. Walsh DATE: 1 / 14 / 80

15.

AGE
35

16.

FIRST NAME						MIDDLE INITIAL	LAST NAME				
T	H	O	M	A	S	P	E	V	A	N	S

17.

NO AND STREET	132 92nd AVENUE	APT 3D
CITY AND STATE	DOLTON MI	ZIP CODE 52435

18.

ADDRESS: 14 Adams Avenue 5F
Number and Street Apt.

Highland CA 91324
City State Zip

HOW LONG AT THIS ADDRESS? 3 yrs. 2 mos.

PREVIOUS ADDRESS: 32 Grant Rd., Middletown, N.J. 19678

19.

NAME: Last: Fodera	First: Robert		M.I. A
ADDRESS: Number and Street: 85 Nelson Avenue			
City, State and Zip: Northbrook, Tx. 84376			
PHONE: (312) 558-8942	DATE OF BIRTH: 8/ 2/51		
SOCIAL SECURITY NUMBER: 215-48-7283			
MARITAL STATUS: ☐ single	☑ married	☐ divorced	
☐ widowed	☐ separated		
SIGNATURE: Robert A. Fodera		DATE: 7/24/81	

20.

NAME	First: DANIEL	M.I.: C	Last: MURPHY
NO. AND STREET	453 MADISON AVENUE		
CITY AND STATE	WATERTOWN FL	ZIP 52364	HOW LONG 2yrs 6mo
PREVIOUS ADDRESS (IF LESS THAN 3 YEARS AT PRESENT)	15 Morrison Street, Glen Ridge, N.H. 23785		
PHONE: (786) 636-0905		DATE OF BIRTH: 3/31/48	
SOCIAL SECURITY NO.: 315481252		MARITAL STATUS: Separated	
SIGNATURE: Daniel C. Murphy		DATE: 9/30/81	

2nd Intermission

Passage 1

1. (c) The statement is a disclaimer. It explains the situations in which a warranty is invalid. Thus, you would find this passage on a product warranty.
2. The passage states that the product is not covered if damages were caused by:
   - abuse, mishandling, neglect, accident, or fire
   - service by anyone other than the manufacturer or an authorized dealer or service center
   - parts supplied by anyone other than the manufacturer or an authorized dealer or service center
3. The passage explains that damages caused by service by anyone other than the manufacturer or an authorized dealer or service center are not covered by the warranty. Thus, you can conclude that in order to make sure the coverage remains in effect, you should take the product to the manufacturer or an authorized dealer or service center for repairs.
4. (c) Based on the information in the passage, you can conclude that the product will be covered only if the manufacturer caused the damage. From this, you can infer that the product would be covered if the manufacturer improperly installed a part.

Passage 2

1. (a) The word *authorize* in the first sentence is a clue that this is a consent statement. Since the passage talks about credit records and credit history, you can conclude that it is a consent statement from an application for a loan.
2. Since the blank comes immediately after *I*, you can infer that the applicant's name is to be filled in on this blank.
3. The passage states that the applicant gives the Bay City Savings and Loan Association permission to investigate the applicant's credit records, to make sure he has not lied on the form, and to check whatever anyone else has said about his ability to repay debts.

Passage 3

1. (b) The second sentence of the passage states that you must buy 4 books.
2. The passage does not tell you what the "regular discount rate" is.
3. The sixth sentence of the passage states that if you want the monthly selection(s), you do not have to do anything.
4. The eighth sentence of the passage states that if you do not want the monthly selection(s), you must mark the order form "no selection" and return it by the date specified on the card.
5. The ninth sentence of the passage states that you have 10 days to make your decision.
6. (b) The passage explains that you have 10 days to decide whether or not you want the monthly selection(s). This means that if you do not want the monthly selection(s), you have 10 days to return the card. From this you can infer that if you do not return the card within 10 days, the book will be sent to you whether you want it or not.

Passage 4

1. (c) The passage is an affirmation statement. Affirmation statements usually are found near the line for your signature.
2. The passage states that the applicant swears that he has not deliberately lied on the application. It also states that if he has lied, the applicant understands that this may cause him to be fired.

Passage 5

1. (d) The passage explains how the finance charge works and how much you have to pay each month. This information would be found on an application for a credit card.
2. (b) The first section of the passage states that if your unpaid balance is less than $300, the finance charge is 2% of your balance. Thus, if your balance were $100, the finance charge would be 2% of $100.
3. (c) The first section of the passage states that the finance charge is 2% of your balance up to $300 and 1% of the part of your balance that is more than $300. Thus, if your balance were $400, the finance charge would be 2% of $300 and 1% of $400-$300, or $100.
4. (b) The second section of the passage explains that the minimum monthly payment is 10% of your average daily balance if your balance is $500 or less. Thus, if your balance were $300, the minimum payment would be 10% of $300.
5. (c) The second section of the passage states that the mimimum payment is 10% of your average daily balance up to $500 and 20% of the part of your average daily balance that is more than $500. Thus, if your balance were $1,000, the minimum payment would be 10% of $500 plus 20% of $1,000 - $500, or $500.

After the Show

Vocabulary Review

1. A *finance charge* is a percentage that is added to the amount you owe on your credit card.
2. To *register* means to submit one's name for things such as voting.
3. A person who is *anemic* suffers from an inadequate amount of red blood cells.
4. A *flier* is a printed sheet of paper that is given out by hand.
5. A *creditor* is a person or institution that lends money.
6. A *primary* is an election among members of one political party.
7. An *ally* is a person or country that cooperates with another person or country.
8. To *consent* means to agree or to give one's permission.

9. *Invalid* means no longer legally acceptable or usable.
10. To *authorize* is to officially approve or permit.
11. *Comprehensive insurance* covers losses caused by fire and theft.
12. *Outstanding* means not yet paid.
13. *The polls* is the place where one goes to vote.
14. An *applicant* is one who applies for, or requests, something.
15. *Party affiliation* means the political party you support.
16. A *platform* is a political party's positions on the issues.
17. *Liability insurance* covers injuries to others and damage to property.
18. *Cast my ballot* means to give in my vote.

Reading Skills Review

Exercise 2

1. According to section 5 of the instructions, a person who has previously registered should fill out the form if he has moved or has failed to vote in at least one election during the past two years.
2. Section 4 of the instructions states that the county board of elections must receive the completed form no later than 30 days before the election.
3. In the "absentee ballot" section, the passage states that a person can get an absentee ballot if he is sick, physically disabled, or out of his county of residence on election day.
4. On line 1, you would fill in:

Last Name	First Name	Initial	Jr. or Sr.
Diamond	Marion	C	

5. If you had never before been a registered voter in this state, you would simply check "no" in section 4.
6. On line 3 you would fill in:

Date of birth	Sex	Height	Color of eyes
		5ft 4in	

7. If you wanted to vote in the upcoming Democratic primary, you would have to check "Democratic" in section 6. This is explained in section 7 of the instructions.
8. On the line marked *Registration Signature* you would fill in:

REGISTRATION SIGNATURE ⟹	X	Marion C. Diamond

Exercise 3

1. On line 5 you would fill in:

Herman Sawyer
(SIGNATURE OF PATIENT)

This is the only part of the form that asks for the patient's name.

2. On the line labeled 1, you would fill in the name *Paul Lederman.*
3. (b) The type of operation would be filled in immediately after the words *the following operation or procedure*. Thus, the word *tonsillectomy* would be filled in on the line labeled 2.
4. (c) The name of the doctor would be filled in on the line immediately following the words *were explained to me by Dr*. Thus, *Lederman* (or *Paul Lederman*) would be filled in on the line labeled 3.
5. This line explains that the patient understands that there is no guarantee that the operation will be a success.
6. (c) The passage explains that the patient gives the doctor permission to use whatever anesthetics are necessary.

Exercise 4

1. On line 2 you would fill in:

Last Name	First Name	Middle Initial
Gregory	Elizabeth	M.

2. This information should be filled in on the line for the name of applicant 2. This is line 13.
3. On line 1 you would fill in:

Amount Requested	Reason
$ 2,500	To buy a used car

4. On lines 7-8, you would fill in:

Employer's Name	Employed Since Mo Yr
Union Grocers	8/79
Employer's Address	**Work Phone & Ext**
17 Main Street, Union City, Alabama 61534	(613) 532-1764

5. On line 3 you would fill in:

Residence Purchase Price	$
Present Value	$ 45,000

6. On line 18 you would fill in:

My take home pay (excluding overtime)	$ 725 monthly

7. On line 31 you would fill in:

STORE ACCTS				
Franklin's Department Store—Union City, AL	6314725	$35	$375	

8. On line 11 you would fill in:

Auto Insurance	Expires Mo./Yr.
Type Liability	
Company Home Mutual	12/84

9. (d) Line 45 is in the part of the form that is marked *Office Use Only*. Thus, you should not make any marks on this line.

Exercise 5

1. In sections 1, 2, 3, 5, and 7, you would fill in:

1. Full Name of Proposed Insured (Print First, Middle and Last Name)			2. Social Security No.
Susan Ann Galindez			131-58-9229
3. Birthdate (Mo.-Day-Yr.) 9/5/39	4. Sex ☐ M ☑ F	5. Birthplace Brooklyn, N.Y.	6. Issue Policy At Age
7. Residence Address (Give Street and Number, City or Town, State and Zip Code) 179 9th Avenue, Brooklyn, N.Y. 10229			

2. In sections 8 and 9 you would fill in:

8. A. Employer and Kind of Business	9. A. Occupation
Galaxy Shoe Manufacturers—shoe manufacturer	Secretary
B. Business Address 175 Cedarview Drive Brooklyn, N.Y. 10342	B. How Long in Present Occupation? 15 years C. Any Change Contemplated? Yes ☐ No ☑ (If "Yes" Explain in Remarks)

3. In sections 10, 11, and 14A, you would fill in:

10. Plan	11. Amount	14A. Premium Interval
Whole Life	$50,000	☐ Annual - 12 Months ☐ Semi Annual - 6 Months ☑ Quarterly - 3 Months ☐ Monthly - 1 Month ☐ COM - 1 Month

4. According to the instructions in section 18, first beneficiaries share the insurance money equally. Thus, in section 18 you would fill in:

18. Beneficiary: (Give full names, dates of birth and relationships to Proposed Insured)

First William Galindez, 6/29/37, husband
Stephanie Galindez, 11/12/63, daughter

Second

Payment will be shared equally by all first beneficiaries who survive insured; if none, by all second beneficiaries who so survive; if none, payment will be made to owner or executors or administrators of the owner's estate.

☐ As per supplemental request

The right to change the beneficiary is reserved.

5. (d) According to the instructions, if you are applying for life insurance, you should fill in questions 1-9 and questions 10-28. Thus, you would not fill in section 29.
6. (b) According to the instructions, if you are applying for disability insurance, you should fill in questions 1-9 and 20-39. Thus, you would not fill out section 10.
7. This sentence explains that the applicant allows anyone with information about the applicant's health to give this information to the insurance company.